A
Taste
OF
HEAVEN

REDISCOVERING
A NEW DIMENSION
OF OUR RELATIONSHIP
WITH GOD – A TRUE
NEARNESS OF HEAVEN
ON EARTH

MARTIN H. MEYER

WESTBOW
PRESS®
A DIVISION OF THOMAS NELSON
& ZONDERVAN

This book is a work of non-fiction. Unless otherwise noted, the author and the publisher make no explicit guarantees as to the accuracy of the information contained in this book and in some cases, names of people and places have been altered to protect their privacy.

WestBow Press books may be ordered through booksellers or by contacting:

WestBow Press
A Division of Thomas Nelson & Zondervan
1663 Liberty Drive
Bloomington, IN 47403
www.westbowpress.com
844-714-3454

ISBN: 979-8-3850-2492-6 (sc)
ISBN: 979-8-3850-2494-0 (hc)
ISBN: 979-8-3850-2493-3 (e)

Library of Congress Control Number: 2024909009

Print information available on the last page.

WestBow Press rev. date: 05/22/2024

My little heaven is here on earth, in the place of blissful intimacy with the Holy Spirit.

Contents

Contents

Introduction

The thought of writing this book was definitely not my own, because if it had been, I would never have undertaken it. I was inspired to write this book as I felt God telling me to share the things that He endows me with from His grace. In God's heart there is a great longing for all Christians to know and experience a taste of heaven here on earth. God's desire is that hearts in the church of Christ may be open for something new – to know Him in a new dimension, which has been veiled and unknown before.

When a few years ago, God revealed His glory to me, the way I prayed totally changed. I stopped worrying about using 'proper' words; I simply started to spend time with the Lord. When we function on the basis of this principle and treat prayer as an encounter with our Father, our perspective on Christianity completely changes. Faith is no longer a struggle and fight against doubt. Prayer is no longer a boring monolog but starts to be the most fascinating thing in our lives. The Holy Spirit descends on us with His glory and brings with Him a piece of heaven. In these moments there is no such thing that could be more real than Jesus, there is nothing we could long for more, and there is nothing we could want more – Jesus becomes everything.

Currently there are many believers who were brought up in Christian families that feel inferior, saying they do not have a great testimony of conversion as others. The book *"A Taste of Heaven"* responds to these kind of doubts, since the greatest testimony of any Christian is not the number and amount of sins committed in the past, but their relationship with God, as a person – the solid fact, who He is for us *today*.

Within Solomon's temple, the 'Holy Place' was the place which directly preceded the Holy of Holies – and God has exactly this type of place for each of us – the place of closeness and reality, when the doors of heaven are wide open and the glory flowing from that place pierces through our whole being.

God led me to such place, where I collided with such intense glory, glory which my body could hardly bear. I wanted to die and be with the Lord. It was something incredibly strong, real and dramatic. I cried to the Lord: *Please, kill me, because I want to be with You now Lord. Kill me, please kill me"*. When the glory of heaven descends on us, we are instantly aware of our imperfections and we receive the revelation of eternity, we long to be with the Lord. However, God needs us to be His representatives, the ones, who carry the atmosphere of heaven whenever we go.

When we encounter the reality of heaven, our hearts begin to burn with desperation to live in intimacy with God, in order to know Him more. Our image of earthly pleasures, as something that has any meaning, is totally ruined. The taste of heaven changes our life completely – heaven sets an indelible mark in our hearts. From that moment on there is no such thing, which may be stronger than God and there is nothing we crave for more.

A Taste of Heaven is a book, which will encourage you to seek a personal God, and create in our hearts desperation to collide with His glory. This book confirms that God, in a great and profound way, rewards all those that search for Him.

It is also crucial to see the personhood of the Holy Spirit, which is the result of relationship with Him. Fellowship with God is not only important for each of us, but it is also something we can freely build our faith on. On many occasions we hear that emotions are not the basis of our faith, because the foundation is only the Word of God, and all of the feelings, emotions and experiences are relative and subjective. It is an extremely religious comprehension of Christianity. My thesis is something completely different: the Word of God is not a denial and disapproval of God's personality, but is its infinite revelation. Thus, fellowship with the Holy Spirit is something which strengthens and builds our faith, making the Word of God alive.

A Taste of Heaven is also a book about many of my experiences with the Holy Spirit. Although they are very personal, I believe God does not expect me to keep them only for myself. Our Lord longs to see the whole Church desiring to know Him in a close and tangible way.

After God revealed to me a piece of heaven, my whole Christian perspective drastically changed. As a result I started to see God as a person completely separated from religion. I started to treat Him as my Father and my best friend. The whole world became for me only a shadow of the things to come, because knowing the glory of God always turns our life upside-down. We start to turn away from worldliness and begin to desire to imprint our life in eternity.

This book is a picture of what is taking place in the inner being of the man who acknowledges the real glory of the Lord. It is also encouragement for everyone to begin to dine with the Lord and have our own secrets with Him.

My prayer is that everyone, after reading this book, may crave for a touch of the glory of heaven and would be inspired to start the journey of seeking his own piece of heaven.

> *Eye has not seen, nor ear heard, and what does not have entered into the human heart, that God has prepared for those who love him. For God has revealed to us by his Spirit: for the Spirit searches all things, even the deep things of God (1 Corinthians 2:9-10).*

But what things were gain to me, these things I have counted as loss for Christ. Yet indeed I also count all things loss for the excellence of the knowledge of Christ Jesus my Lord, for whom I have suffered the loss of all things, and count them as rubbish, that I may gain Christ (…) I press toward the goal for the prize of the upward call of God in Christ Jesus.

(Philippians 3:7-8,14, NKJV)

1

THE GREATEST ABSURDITY
OF RELIGION

*Religion without God as a person is the
same philosophy as anything else.*

T he story of my life is different from what is commonly read
in Christian books. I cannot say I belong to the noble group
of people which can talk for hours about their horrific past
full of mistakes and failures which they regret up to this day. I am
not one of those who can boast of a spectacular story of conversion.

I was brought up in a Protestant family. I regularly attended
church. I cannot say I was once very evil and now I am good and
virtuous. I was a normal, energetic boy. I liked to sing old hymns.
In the evenings I knelt beside the bed to pray. When I was five years
old, along with my twin brother we accepted the Lord Jesus into our
hearts. When I was nine years old, I had read the entire Bible and I
could name, from memory, all of its books.

It seemed that my life did not lack anything, I was a child
surrounded by happiness and devoted to Jesus, faithful in all the
things religion demands. But as I grew up, something began to
change. I looked at what surrounded me, and I asked myself: "Is there
any meaning in this? Is there something real and alive? Am I for the

rest of my life doomed to not knowing the God in whom I believe and told about so often?".

In my childish thinking I was very frank and honest. I just wanted to see the God to whom I prayed so earnestly. I wanted to know the one to whom I sang. I wanted to touch Him and to feel His touch. Everyone told me that God is not a figment of our imagination, but He is a real person. So why can't I see Him? Why can't I talk to Him? Will I be limited throughout all of my days only to hear about God everyone has talked about so much?

It was then, in these young years of childhood, full of joy, adventure and school frolics, there began to be born in my heart a hunger for knowing God. I did not spend hours in prayer or fast for weeks. I simply lived. I was a pretty ordinary boy, eager for adventure, new experiences and surrounded by friends in school. There was nothing extraordinary about me, but God had placed in my heart a desire to know Him. In the next few years this small, insignificant feeling became a flame that possessed my whole heart. From that moment on I was never going to stop wanting to seek after God - to meet Him and to get to know who He really is.

Sometimes, when I remember all these years, which could be considered the worst in my life, I feel the presence of the Holy Spirit. I know that when I was a completely unaware ten years old boy, God was by my side. He was with me all that time. He cared for me, loved me and protected me.

My earthly father was not the perfect example of what paternity is. I recall the times when he took me and my brother to places children should not go. My mother then was in England, working hard to earn the money we needed so much during that time. Now I know that God had everything carefully planned. Everything had a purpose, even that which seemed hard to understand at the time.

Some years after that I went as usual to the Sunday church service. It all started as normal: people singing, announcements and taking the offering. And then our pastor said:

"If anyone wants to thank God for something, please step forward, take the microphone and pray". I started to think very intensely. What could I thank God for? Is there anything for which I could express my gratitude to Him? And then God came to me. Right in the middle of the service. For the first time in my life I felt Him. I burst into tears. God showed me the things for which I could thank Him. Then He took me with Him on a journey through my past. He showed me all the times when I was alone. He showed me the days when I was without a father, without a mother, without the things that every child so desperately needs - love, acceptance and understanding. I felt it very clearly. God was with me when I did not have a dad. He was my Daddy!

It was then, during a normal church service, God in a moment showed me that through all the years He was there with me. He stood by my side, to soothe the pain and to whisper to my heart the words that I needed so much: "I love you, my dear child. You are very precious to me. Keep in mind that I was always there with you. I'm your Daddy.". When I heard that, I could not get up. God's presence filled that place. I sat curled up on my chair, flooding with tears. I could not utter a single word. I couldn't move. My body strangely trembled. I felt a heat I had never felt before. My heavenly Father was with me and was telling me that He loved me so much. I knew that if I could somehow get to the microphone to say something, I would only cry. God's presence flooded that place with great force and intensity. I also knew that I could not express in any way the gratitude for who my Father is and that I will never be able to do so. God's love is far beyond my comprehension.

I was sixteen years old when something had begun. I was sure that it would not end. My Daddy was with me. He was always with me. I left the church service filled with new freshness and new desires. It was not the baptism in the Holy Spirit and I also didn't receive the gift of tongues. God just entered in and embraced me. That's all. Nothing great or mystical happened. No thunder sounded from heaven nor did a multitude of angels appear to me. My heavenly Father came to me and hugged me. That's all, but it was so much.

This was the beginning of my pursuit after God. After this experience my desire began to deepen. I wanted to know God even closer. I could not limit myself to only one experience. Later, God has taught me that He is grieved when we limit ourselves to just one experience with Him. What's more, everything we receive from Him is not because of our merit but only His response to our hunger.

Sometimes I hear the testimonies of people who talk for hours about their terrible and sinful past and spend just a moment talking about their conversion – one moment with God. At such times there rises in my heart a cry, "Lord, give us, the Church, people full of experiences of You, people of faith and intimacy, those who know the taste of Your glory.". How much I long for the time when our testimonies will be filled with stories about our Daddy, the Holy Spirit and Jesus. How I would love to hear about God, who when He comes, all the scars of the past, all of the pains and unhealed wounds are instantly erased from our hearts, along with condemnation and unforgiveness.

God is waiting for the moment when we will stop hiding and start affecting everyone around us with the passion of knowing Him. The time when we will begin to share with others what He has given us, and what lies ahead undiscovered.

But there is something that effectively prevents us against coming into this new dimension of relationship with the Father. It is human arrogance and pride. Whenever I heard about people who were used mightily by God, I always said: "Lord, why don't I have what they had? I don't have it but I want to get it and I will do anything to have it.".

God is waiting for the time when His church will humble itself and say: "I want what Elijah, the apostles Peter and Paul, Smith Wigglesworth, brother Allen, John G. Lake, Kathryn Kuhlman and dozens of other servants of God had, who were so humble that God could fulfill His purpose for them.". The Bible says "God opposes the proud, but gives grace to the humble" (James 4:6, ESV).

This is a mystery in which God begins to give us His grace when we accept and begin to live its revelation.

The issue of grace is often underestimated. Everything we receive, own and have, we owe to God's grace. The more grace we have, the closer we are to Jesus. Grace is the key to God's world, full of new revelations of God – a world closed for many.

I have heard several times that God gives grace according to the quality of our character; God looks in places where no one else can look. But the Bible states something different. God gives grace to those who are *humble*. True humility releases true greatness, and this is the complete biblical truth.

When we are humble, we enter into an intimate relationship with God, and when we reach it, we will always display a godly character - even if no one sees us.

Real humility is more valuable than human approval. Humility is nothing else but giving first place to God – becoming smaller, so that the Lord can become greater - in every decision of our life.

The Lord has prepared something special for everyone. I am sure He has a destiny planned for each of us. I do not agree with the fact that God calls some people to great things, and others to some smaller ones. My God is a God of great things and He has something special for everyone. But we must remember that everyone is called to *different* great things. Not everyone can be a minister or pastor, while also not every pastor and preacher can be a good administrator, businessman or psychologist. Greatness is not always what we think it is. God has His own definition of greatness and for each of us greatness may be something completely different. The key is hidden in being in the center of His calling and will.

The Most High does not look at our titles or the positions we hold. The most important thing is our desire to be with him. Our abiding in His presence is what God desires the most. For Him it does not matter whether you are or aren't a pastor, apostle or prophet.

Over the past few years I have been looking at the church and I wonder if we see Jesus as a personal friend. It is very sad that Jesus is so often deprived of His personality. He becomes the Jesus who, when he touches, nothing changes. Jesus, whose presence is hard to define or feel. Jesus, whose glory is something distant, unreal and reserved for the life after death. An impersonal Jesus is the greatest absurdity of religion. I do not believe in that Jesus and I do not know such.

I don't want Christianity to be based on the ideology that says the Holy Spirit cannot meet with me, embrace me or *pour* His love upon me. If this were to be the God of Christianity, there would be nothing in Christianity which would be worthy of living for. The Holy Spirit is not an ideology or a philosophy of life. He is a true *person*. By God's grace I know Him *personally*, and Jesus is my only Truth. God's Word says:

> *But now in Christ Jesus, you who once were [so] far away, through (by, in) the blood of Christ have been brought near. For He is [Himself] our peace (our bond of unity and harmony) ... For it is through Him that we both [whether far off or near] now have an introduction (access) by one [Holy] Spirit to the Father [so that we are able to approach Him].* (Ephesians 2:13–14a, 18, AMP).

Through the blood of Jesus we have the freedom to come to *His closeness*! At this point the question arises: What is *God's closeness*? Religion teaches us that *it may be something but as well it may be nothing*.

But how is it possible that closeness may be undefined? When we meet with our fiancée is it possible to feel nothing or treat her like the air? Can we pass by our beloved without any affection? Surely not. And so it is with the Holy Spirit. He is not some mysterious and inaccessible power. He is a real person. His touch is a real touch. His arms embrace us and soothe any pain. His voice is sweet and true. His heart feels the same way as the heart of every man. He can be sad and angry, He can laugh and shed tears, He can veil His face, and He can unveil it, He speaks and sings. His nearness is real and can be felt – it is more real and closer than the presence of any human being.

I remember to this day when I said to God: "If You really exist, I want to feel You, regardless of the price I would have to pay! I want to experience Your power and collide with Your reality. Reveal Yourself to me!"

When we say these kinds of words, God treats them very seriously, and His answer will only depend on the size of our desire, hunger and determination. My desire was huge. It turned into a cry of desperation and became a constant shout of my heart. Then the Lord taught me a lesson. He made me aware that He will never be a man, because He is our Creator. However, this does not mean that there has to be distance between us. God created me so that I may know Him in a full and perfect way. How is it possible for me to get to know the person who is not and never will be a man? Only by the Spirit[1].

Despite how it appears, this is not difficult. The more we meet with God, the more we get to know the spiritual world as well as the rules and laws through which that world is governed. The more we spend time with the Holy Spirit, the more we are sensitive and aware of the spiritual world.

The Bible teaches us that man is spirit, has a soul and lives in a body. How difficult it is to live being more aware of the reality of the spirit than what is of the body; to see through spiritual eyes, to hear with spiritual ears, to listen with the heart and speak the language of the spirit. How difficult it is! One of the first passages of Scripture I memorized was the one where God is speaking about this principle:

> *Since you have been raised to new life with Christ, set your sights on the realities of heaven, where Christ sits in the place of honor at God's right hand. Think about the things of heaven, not the things of earth. For you died to this life, and your real life is hidden with Christ in God.* (Colossians 3:1-3, NLT).

God can sometimes really surprise us. This passage speaks about our new birth. Our old self died and we received a new spirit. The Bible also says that from that time on we will never die because we have passed from death to eternal life. This is a great biblical truth,

---

[1]   And obviously through the Son of Man, Jesus Christ who came to this world in the form of human flesh so that we can have relationship with God. He was fully man and fully God. Thus through Him and Him only we have access to God.

possible to understand only from the perspective of the heart, not the mind.

There will surely come the day when I will have to say goodbye to this world. Will it be sad? For many people yes. But when I think of heaven, I recall the words of Saint Paul, that death is a gain for him. He said that because he knew heaven! He knew the taste of the glory of heaven. Thus, there was an apparent struggle in his heart - he longed to be already with the Lord, without this earthly, imperfect body. But at the same time he knew that there was so much to do here - on the earth. This is what Jesus desires for all of us — to know a taste of heaven, marked by a great longing for Him.

When I was seventeen, I was baptized in the Holy Spirit and the Holy Spirit gave me a new language. I remember that day as if it were today. I took it very seriously. I said to myself: "If God gave me something so amazing, it has to be incredibly important to me.". I hid in the closet and waited until everyone had left the house so that I could listen to these strange words that were coming out of my mouth. Words accompanied by a great deal of emotions. I was excited and aroused.

That was when I fell in love with prayer. I decided that I would pray at least an hour each day. I would go to the church an hour and a half before my classes. I sang, prayed in the Holy Spirit, screamed and jumped. I did everything I wanted. I was free before my Lord. I was glad that I was with Him and He was even gladder that I was with Him. A strong bond was created between us.

We often hear that only we can enjoy God's presence. However, what really counts is that God could enjoy our presence. When we begin to understand of our relationship with God this way our Christian perspective completely changes. We desire to give Jesus every free moment of our life so that not only we would enjoy His presence but that He could also rejoice with us. Just like a newly engaged couple. We miss the Holy Spirit whenever we do anything that interrupts us in thinking about Him, and we want to return to the place where it is just us and Him.

After I was baptized, the Lord began to shape a desire in my heart to be devoted to Him. I will never forget those precious moments in high school, when I prayed with my brother and school friends during the long breaks. We prayed about everything. The Lord heard us and gave us even more of his grace. I will never forget the times when a few people from my church met in the evenings and we spent the whole nights singing, praying and just being with Jesus – simply enjoying His precious presence.

Today, when I look at those years when I was discovering I can pray while chewing gum, taking a shower, riding an elevator or even sitting on the toilet, I can only smile. God does not live with us on a bodily level and it does not matter to Him if we are driving a car, taking a shower or doing things that we would be ashamed of before people.

When I was nineteen I had to deal with a major dilemma. I had to decide which course of study to choose. It was a serious decision that had a great deal of importance for my future. However, inside my heart I knew that the Lord wanted to give me even more of Himself. Like any teenager, I was filled with many new ideas. I thought about almost everything: from foreign Bible schools, to the academy of physical education, English literature and various theological seminaries.

All the people around me agreed that I should go to Bible school because they believed that one day I would be a pastor. I remember, while thinking about that option, I received a very clear picture from the Holy Spirit. He showed me the best car I could ever have imagined, and he said: "If you received such a car, would you prefer to learn about it or get into it and start driving?" The Holy Spirit spoke to me through an ordinary example.

I decided then that I would not spend the next few years learning about the car standing in front of me, since I could get inside and start learning how to drive it, to learn it from the inside, to experience the excitement of driving and enjoy the fullness of its possibilities.

That was a decision. I told God that I did not want to learn about Him, but wanted to know Him - to find out who He really is. So I decided to go to college part-time, and dedicate all my free time to seeking God. I made the next step.

God saw my hunger. I did not care for education, for a good future, making a great career. I wanted to know the reality of God, in whom I believed. I also knew that He would take care of all of the rest. I decided to devote three years to cry out to God: "Lord, please let me know who you really are.". I did not have to wait for the answer long. A few months later God allowed me to collide with His real glory and power. He allowed me to know Him personally.

God gives each of us a choice: we can limit ourselves to listen to some sermons about Jesus, hearing stories about Him; we can also study hundreds of theological books and know all the books of the Bible by heart. We can fulfill all the things religion demands - to pray regularly, read a few chapters of the Bible every day and sing some beautiful worship songs. We may find ourselves in a place where we will have fulfilled all of our duties.

However, the knowledge of the Lord lies not only in fulfilling duties but in true and sincere desire of the heart. Jesus said: *These you ought to have done, without leaving the others undone.*[2] So it will not be sufficient to do what the church tells us to do. Our Lord is looking for people to whom He will reveal Himself in a new dimension: supernatural and divine.

In this world so many people live full of doubt and unbelief, who think that Christianity is boring. They say that the churches are filled with empty celebration and rituals and there is nothing real and alive.

But no matter what place you are in today, God has for you something completely new. He wants to let you know Him in a dimension you did not know before. He wants to show you heaven. The Lord is waiting for the day when you say: "Lord, please let me know who you really are!". If it is a sincere and genuine desire, God will reveal Himself to you in a way you did not expect or even dream of – He will let you

---

[2]   Matthew 23:23, KJV

know Him as a real person. You will quickly begin to discover how fascinating and wonderful life with Jesus can be.

In the next chapter we will discuss experiences with God. We will explain what they are, and reflect on their role and importance in our Christian life.

Prayer

(Lyrics: Third Day, Nothing Compares)

I've heard all the stories
I've seen all the signs
Witnessed all the glory
Tasted all that's fine

But nothing compares
To the greatness of knowing You Lord
Oh, no, nothing compares
To the greatness of knowing You Lord

STUDY QUESTIONS

➢ What is the greatest absurdity of religion? Do you see some other absurdities? Which ones?

➢ To whom does God give His grace?

➢ What attitude displays real humility and which are the effects of having a humble heart?

➢ What is the difference between the image of God you are told by people and the God you know *personally*?

➢ Have you ever said to God: "Lord, please show me who you really are"?

I cry aloud to God,
   aloud to God; and he hears me.
   On the day of my distress I am seeking *Adonai*;
my hands are lifted up;
my tears flow all night without ceasing;
my heart refuses comfort.
When remembering God, I moan;
when I ponder, my spirit fails. *(Selah)*
You hold my eyelids [and keep me from sleeping];
I am too troubled to speak.
I think about the days of old,
the years of long ago;
in the night I remember my song,
I commune with myself, my spirit inquires:
"Will *Adonai* reject forever?
will he never show his favor again?
I will meditate on your work
and think about what you have done.
God, your way is in holiness.
What god is as great as God?
You are the God who does wonders,
you revealed your strength to the peoples.
With your arm you redeemed your people,
the descendants of Jacob and Joseph (…)
The sound of your thunder was in the whirlwind,
the lightning flashes lit up the world,
the earth trembled and shook.
(Psalm 77:1-7, 12-16, 19, *Complete Jewish Bible*)

2

EXPERIENCES WITH GOD

There are moments that no one is able to give you
and no one can take them away from you – these
are the moments spent in the reality of heaven.

O ne of the great wonders of life with Jesus is that there are many experiences that no one knows about aside from Him. These arise only in places where there are hungry hearts that are not satisfied with commonness and routine.

God, in response to the hunger He saw in my heart, began to reveal what I really wanted - the beauty of His closeness. He saw my heart, when I had said I would not spend the next few years learning about Him from books, lectures and theological textbooks, but I wanted to know Him personally. I was certain that I would receive the answer.

However, before the Lord began to reveal to me His glory, I had to learn a lot. I know that till the end of my days on this earth I will always be learning and my life will be full of surprising revelations and discoveries; like a little baby, still noticing newer and newer things.

When we truly seek God, we will never be left for ourselves. Our Father will be with us, and what is more - it will be accompanied by a lot of unusual experiences, because it is these which are worth living for.

I cannot imagine Christianity without wonderful and beautiful moments spent with Jesus. Without tears, sometimes endlessly flowing down my face, without shouts, often so excruciating and piercing that it seems they move all of heaven. I cannot imagine life without the countless nights spent alone with the Holy Spirit, without His warm voice, without the love of heaven, and the melody of the Spirit. I cannot imagine my Christianity without dozens or even hundreds of secrets with my Lord. I cannot imagine my life without the experiences of Him.

Whenever I look back, I see grace. I will never say that something is indebted to myself or that something is due to my discipline. I will never let myself look back and in arrogance and pride recall all those times when He was so tangibly close.

My heart cries when I see how religion tries to rob the church of the things that are priceless for me. I cannot imagine that someone could question what is the essence of my life, which gives me encouragement, awakens faith and enlivens hope.

Experiences are what give our life a purpose, it stimulates in us gratitude and love, allowing us to survive when we are weak; and more – they are these moments which only our Lord knows, our sweet secrets with Him.

Sometimes there comes a doubt and feeling that something will not succeed, that I won't be able to cope, that people will not understand, that it will be the end. There comes a time when everything around begins to lose its charm and splendor. I start to forget how joy and peace taste. Dreams grow weak and the future seems to be uncertain. Then, when hope is barely smoldering and faith is down to its last ounce of strength, recollection of experiences kindle in me the same fire that was burning when I felt God's nearness so strong. I wonder what I would do if I did not have those moments, if I had nothing to look back at or recall.

In our lives there are some moments that no one is able to give us and no one can take them away from us, because these are the moments spent in the reality of heaven. There are some things that we should not speak or write about, because we will not be able to fully express what we experienced or felt.

My first prayers were not full of excitement and dedication. In my heart I was aware that it would not be so forever. However, deep in my heart I knew that one day something would start to happen, that finally I would begin to sense God's closeness. I have never agreed with the view that prayer is only a time of contemplation and meditation. I knew that, although I was not experiencing any mystical sensations, in my heart great changes were taking place. I believed the Word.

Just like you, I have heard hundreds of sermons that emphasized how important a time of prayer is for Christians. I took it seriously, and I told myself that if this is so. I will pray, whatever that means. Beginning was not easy. So many times I would close my eyes and try to pray, but after a few minutes I find that my thoughts had wandered in a completely different direction. So many times, sitting in the church early in the morning, I fought with my weak body, trying to stop myself from falling to sleep. Sometimes I even succeeded. So many times when going to the church at night to pray, I would eat sweets and drink coffee while my mind wandered in its own paths. This was not the kind of prayer that I had heard about – the kind of prayer where servants of God, who during their conversations with God, were accompanied by such an intense presence of God that it was not possible to enter the room they prayed without falling to one's knees.

Nevertheless, I did not give up and I never ceased to call for more, because in spite of the struggles and frequent battles with the weakness of my body, I knew that for my Lord, every second of my shallow and imperfect prayer was extremely precious. I was sure, that after time, maybe in a few months or years, God would respond. He would give me something I did not expect or even dreamed of. He would begin to reveal to me His secrets; He would reveal to me the reality of His glory. It would create a bond that nothing and no one will be able to move. I wanted that the most. If my God is alive, and if He is the same God who I read about in the Bible, He will certainly do it.

It is crucial to have unshakable confidence that God sees your every tear, hears every whisper and sigh, and is beside you even in the moments of imperfect beginnings. He cries when you cry. He is glad when you rejoice. He loves to listen to the melodies flowing from our spirit, and sometimes even sings along with us.

At this point, I am reminded of a special prayer. Although I have never been musically talented, I always felt that music is something through which it is easier to express love, to sing out our cares and to calm our souls. I remember one evening when, as usual, I came to the chapel late at night. I walked up the stairs, knelt down and began to sing. I allowed my heart to sing out what it felt.

And then, as I sang, at one point I felt I had heard a voice in my spirit. The words were: "It is I singing for you – just listen.". I was very moved and amazed. How could it be? Could it be God singing? I was not sure, but I let the Holy Spirit continue.

I allowed the Holy Spirit to sing and listened to the words. They were very simple:

"I love you, do not be afraid. I love you, do not be afraid". These words repeated several dozen times.

The feeling of peace I felt was different than any peace I had known before. It was the peace of heaven. It was the kind of peace that could not be touched or moved by any storm, wind or power – even death.

I had such a great certainty that it is impossible to express it in words. From that moment I was absolutely sure that fear would no longer have even the slightest impact on my life. Even death could not change that. So strong was the feeling.

Our experiences with God are reserved only for us. We may share them with others, but we cannot guarantee that others will understand or feel what we do. We cannot guarantee anyone that he will feel what we feel. We do not know what the Holy Spirit will do next, because His ways of acting, speaking and touching are endless. He is infinite in His love.

This is one of the secrets of relationship with Jesus. For each person He gives what is best at any given time and place. Therefore, we cannot expect that the way that the Spirit *manifests* Himself will become a form. Religion creates boxes and drawers to enclose the Holy Spirit, but He never works in a limited way. For God is not a religion, but a Person.

Jesus is sad when we say, "Come, but on our terms". Our beloved Helper and Comforter is waiting for the opposite words, "Come just as you like. I give you, Jesus, complete freedom".

This attitude is what the Lord loves the most. If the heart is not open, nothing happens. This has become a great slogan, but what does it mean to have an open heart?

What is an open heart? There is a story in the Bible that illustrates this perfectly.

> *And behold, a woman of Canaan came from that region and cried out to Him, saying, "Have mercy on me, O Lord, Son of David! My daughter is severely demon-possessed." But He answered her not a word. And His disciples came and urged Him, saying, "Send her away, for she cries out after us." But He answered and said, "I was not sent except to the lost sheep of the house of Israel." Then she came and worshiped Him, saying, "Lord, help me!" But He answered and said, "It is not good to take the children's bread and throw it to the little dogs." And she said, "Yes, Lord, yet even the little dogs eat the crumbs which fall from their masters' table." (Matthew 15:22-27, NKJV)*

This story carries a lot of great messages, but what captivates me the most is this woman's open heart. Today, many of us quickly fall into despair and say: "Well, in that case, there is no chance". But this woman was different. She had an open heart. Her pride was not hurt. She was ready to accept anything and receive everything. She was ready to give anything and to answer any question. And despite the fact that the Lord three times had given her a clear signal that her request went beyond the limits of His mission, she did not give up. She did not lose heart. Oh yes! Her faith was greater than any form.

Yes, Jesus was sent primarily to the people of Israel, but He did not say this to express His resentment against pagans. He said this in order to check her heart.

Openness is the willingness to break through the boundaries of our faith, to give up its stereotypes, to overthrow schematic thinking, to resign from our pride and admit our weakness. Openness of the heart is the gateway to the Spirit - an invitation to intimacy.

Further we read something like this:

> Then Jesus answered and said to her, "O woman, great is your faith! Let it be to you as you desire." And her daughter was healed from that very hour. (Matthew 15:28, NKJV)

If this woman's heart had not open, she wouldn't have received anything. If I was not open, I would have never met my Lord. The boundaries of faith would never be exceeded. I would never know the Lord. I would know a god of religion and not the God of relationship. I would know a god of schematic thinking and the Holy Spirit would only move in the ways I had been told. That is why it is so important.

I thank my God that He taught me that lesson. He showed me that openness always requires dedication and willingness to die to self. Sometimes it even demands that we feel the taste of embarrassment. But is it too high a price to pay for the desire to know the Lord, and for receiving the answer to the cry of our hearts: "Lord! Come down and let me know who you are"? Certainly not.

Less than a year after I was baptized in the Holy Spirit, during a church service, God showed me the spiritual state of the Church. At that moment He let me know by his Spirit the real heart of Jesus, burning with love and longing for His bride. Since then I could never look at the Church without love. God even let me feel His love physically. Even though my heart was filled with deep sadness because of Jesus' great longing for intimacy with the bride, there was never a shortage of love. I began to pray for the Church as the whole body.

The Lord did not show me my fellowship or a few people. He did not show me the differences between some members of our congregation. He did not lift up some or humiliate others. No. He did not do that. The Lord showed me the *Church*. I will never forget the words I felt in my spirit:

"Who will pray if you do not do this?". From my eyes tears began to flow. I ran away from the main hall and hid in another room, to feel comfortable in what God was doing, that His sweet presence may not go away. That moment completely changed my comprehension of the Church.

At that time God instilled in me something from His heart. He placed in me His desires and showed what He wants to give us, as His Church. Since then prayer was not a burden for me, but a pleasure. I wanted to spend every spare second with my Lord. I no longer prayed: "Lord, change them!" but "Lord, change us! Lord, give us something new.". I also wanted something new. Why should I pray for a change for others, not wanting change in myself? I craved for revival. I wanted to be a part of it.

Sometimes I hear the prayer: "Change them. Lord, change this Church. She is in such a terrible place. Change them, O Lord.". These words will never be the prayer of Jesus. He does not want *them*, He wants *us*. *We* are the Bride. However, we will not be able to learn that without knowing Jesus' true love toward His Bride – to the whole Church – and not just chosen ones. Revival does not come in response to the call of individuals, but in the response to a penetrating hunger in our hearts.

A few years ago, something else happened. Once, after a university lecture I came to church and began to pray that God would reveal what is sinful in me. That was because I sensed the ungodliness I lived in. I wanted God to convict me of my sinfulness. I prayed and cried: "Please, show me my sin! Show me my sin! I want to feel it! I want to see it!".

Sometimes we can regret the words we say in prayer, but God never regrets His answers. I didn't say a simple prayer, but it was a scream that permeated my entire being. I wanted change. I craved for holiness. I wanted to feel my sin, to see how I really was. And God answered that prayer, and His answer had a huge impact on my life.

I was screaming for about half an hour and finally God responded – He showed me the weight of my sin. He confronted me with His holiness. My body was literally powerless. In an instant I fell to the floor as if I was dead. I could not utter a word. All I felt was my dirt. God showed me every little imperfection of my heart. He answered my prayer. He gave me what I wanted. I cried with such an intense and penetrating cry that I thought no one had ever cried in that way. I lay howling and my body felt such a huge weight, like a dense layer of frozen snow. I did not have the strength to get up. I was not even able to move! I could not think of anything else. Sin was something cruel and overwhelming. I felt it. It filled my whole being. Every part of my body and soul.

After about an hour, when the weight began to slowly lift, the thought appeared: How did Our Lord feel when He took upon Himself the sin of the whole world? What did the Savior feel when he cried out:

"My God, my God, why hast thou forsaken me?" (Matthew 22,46, KJV). What kind of feeling was it? How did our Lord endure it?

When I finally picked myself up, as I was walking, but every now and then I stopped and fell again. I remember that I managed to get the other room and went the radiator so that I had something to hold on to. For several days I felt this burden physically.

I sat down then at the computer and described everything I felt. I wrote down all of my errors, sins and imperfections. Immediately, I sent a text message to my pastor to tell him that I had something to confess in front of the whole church during the Sunday service. There was nothing terrible to confess. I did not confess any immorality or serious violation of the law. However, God had showed me what is sin by hitting me with His holiness. I felt in my spirit His words: "Only through my blood, you can live.".

At the time I did not understand this, but years later when I looked back, I saw a huge gap between what is sometimes called "holiness" and what true "holiness" really is[3]. Real holiness is the nature of God in us.

When Isaiah collided with God's holiness, he said:

"Woe *is* me, for I am undone! Because I *am* a man of unclean lips, And I dwell in the midst of a people of unclean lips; For my eyes have seen the King, The LORD of hosts."

Then one of the seraphim flew to me, having in his hand a live coal *which* he had taken with the tongs from the altar. And he touched my mouth *with it,* and said:

> *"Behold, this has touched your lips; Your iniquity is taken away, And your sin purged."* (Isaiah 6:5-7, NKJV)

God did not hit Isaiah with His holiness in order to announce to him that his guilt is too great for God to be taken away. God's desire for our closeness is greater than our sin. This picture was, as I believe, a prophetic revelation of the future. I felt in my heart: there will come a day that through the cross that we will be able to see God's glory and feel his intimacy.

It was the same with me. God showed me my sin, not just to prove that I was too vile and unworthy to be able to live with Him, but to give me at least a glimpse of the power of His love. His love is greater than our dirt. His mercy is greater than our weakness and imperfection. His blood is stronger than our sin.

I realized then that God never ever is far from us. Only a person can move away from God, and He is always close no matter how far

---

[3]   Of course there is no way to eliminate from the definition of holiness the quality of our life. The event described above certainly had a huge impact on Isaiah's quality of life. Holiness is the nature of God in us. It contains within itself the desire to do good, and disgust of what is evil - to align ourselves with God's perspective on sin.

we are from Him. It is difficult to understand that without further thinking. However, it is eternal and unchanging truth: the Lord is always near. His love is too great to be able to leave us even for a second.

Since that time I have never prayed with the words: "Lord, come close to me", because I know that He is always near me. When my heart says: "Lord, I come to you through your blood," in a moment His closeness is beside me. How wonderful it is to have this unwavering confidence and to know that the Lord is beside us every second of our lives - ready to respond to the prayer of a child starving for love.

When Jesus departed from this world, He said, "Lo, I am with you always, even unto the end of the world. Amen". (Matthew 28:20, KJV). He gave us a promise that He will always be with us. He did not make any conditions, but placed in the heart of a believer a hundred percent certainty. He left a foundation. This foundation is His always approachable closeness. Full, unwavering, unchanging and unconditional.

In the Gospel of Luke there is a story called the "Parable of the prodigal son":

> And he said, 'A certain man had two sons,
> And the younger of them said to the father, Father, give me
> the portion of the substance falling to [me], and he divided
> to them the living.
> 'And not many days after, having gathered all together,
> the younger son went abroad to a far country, and there he
> scattered his substance, living riotously;
> And he having spent all, there came a mighty famine on that
> country, and himself began to be in want;
> And having gone on, he joined himself to one of the citizens
> of that country, and he sent him to the fields to feed swine,
> And he was desirous to fill his belly from the husks that the
> swine were eating, and no one was giving to him.

'And having come to himself, he said, How many hirelings of my father have a superabundance of bread, and I here with hunger am perishing!
Having risen, I will go on unto my father, and will say to him, Father, I did sin - to the heaven, and before thee,
And no more am I worthy to be called thy son; make me as one of thy hirelings.
'And having risen, he went unto his own father, and he being yet far distant, his father saw him, and was moved with compassion, and having ran he fell upon his neck and kissed him;
And the son said to him, Father, I did sin -- to the heaven, and before thee, and no more am I worthy to be called thy son.
'And the father said unto his servants, Bring forth the first robe, and clothe him, and give a ring for his hand, and sandals for the feet;
And having brought the fatted calf, kill [it], and having eaten, we may be merry,
Because this my son was dead, and did live again, and he was lost, and was found; and they began to be merry.
(Luke 15:11-24a, Young's Literal Translation)

This story is too long to be able to discuss it in detail. Hundreds or even thousands of books, papers and theological expositions have been written on this parable. But there is one thing that touches me the most: the perfect and unconditional love of the Father. At any time I have every right to say: "I'm returning to you, my Father, and I confess that I have sinned against you!". The acceptance of the Father's love only depends on my decision. The love of the Father is constant and unchanging in its character. How wonderful is the love of my Daddy!

Our Father always waits for the return of His child, with every breath hoping that His child will return. He never gives up and is ready at any time, regardless of the status of His child to wrap His arms around us and accept us with His unfailing love! The Lord is always waiting for us with open arms. And whether we will run to Him depends only on our desire.

A year after I was baptized in the Holy Spirit, and a few months afterwards God showed me the spiritual state of the Church, placing in my heart a great desire for revival, I found myself in the same room where I was baptized in the Spirit. I prayed. It was then that the reality of God had become as real as the world I live in. That event changed my life and made me forever in love with the wonders of my Lord. It was the beginning of a holy pursuit for more of the reality of The Most High and His glory.

Is there arising a hunger in your heart to know God's reality? Do you also want, like David, Joseph, Moses, Elijah, Gideon, Esther, Anna and dozens of others of God's servants to have life-changing, transforming experiences with Him? Today is the best day to say to Jesus:

> *God of love and intimacy! Wonderful Savior and the Holy Spirit, my closest friend - I want something new! Refresh me, touch me with a touch I have never experienced before.*

You can be absolutely sure that if your hunger is real and persistent, the Holy Spirit will surprise you and give you something you have not experienced before. You will begin to have your own secrets with Him, sweet and unforgettable moments with the Lord.

In the next chapter we will look at encounters with God. What they are and find out if there was anyone in the Bible who actually met God in all His glory, beauty and truth. So stay with me on the journey!

Prayer

(Lyrics: Rain Down, *Planetshakers*)

I am falling to my knees
I need You Lord to breathe in me
Rain down on me
Rain down on me

Here in Your presence I am free
Pour down like rain
Come and touch me again
Lord let Your presence fall on me

STUDY QUESTIONS

➤ Up till now, how did you get your knowledge about God? Have you learned about God only from Christian books or have you met Him *personally*?

➤ Do you have any of your own experiences with God which you remember in particular? Do you want to have such experiences and why?

➤ What is stronger than your sin and what is greater than your weakness? Do you agree with the fact that God is *always* close to you?

➤ Do you want to have your secrets with the Lord? Would you like to experience with God something you will *never* forget?

J ohn, both your brother and companion in the tribulation and kingdom and patience of Jesus Christ, was on the island that is called Patmos for the word of God and for the testimony of Jesus Christ. I was in the Spirit on the Lord's Day, and I heard behind me a loud voice, as of a trumpet, saying, "I am the Alpha and the Omega, the First and the Last," and, "What you see, write in a book and send it to the seven churches which are in Asia: to Ephesus, to Smyrna, to Pergamos, to Thyatira, to Sardis, to Philadelphia, and to Laodicea." Then I turned to see the voice that spoke with me. And having turned I saw seven golden lampstands, and in the midst of the seven lampstands One like the Son of Man, clothed with a garment down to the feet and girded about the chest with a golden band. His head and hair were white like wool, as white as snow, and His eyes like a flame of fire; His feet were like fine brass, as if refined in a furnace, and His voice as the sound of many waters; He had in His right hand seven stars, out of His mouth went a sharp two-edged sword, and His countenance was like the sun shining in its strength. And when I saw Him, I fell at His feet as dead. But He laid His right hand on me, saying to me, "Do not be afraid; I am the First and the Last. "I am He who lives, and was dead, and behold, I am alive forevermore. Amen. And I have the keys of Hades and of Death." (Revelation 1:9-19, *Modern KJV*)

3

AN ENCOUNTER WITH GOD

*An encounter with God is a time when everything from this world
loses its charm and glare. It is totally torn from any meaning.*

S ince my childhood I have read dozens or even hundreds of
stories about people who have known God in tangible and real
way – people that have met Him. Among them were those who
spent almost their whole lives on their knees, sacrificing themselves
in prayer; there were also preachers who resigned from having a
family, others left their homelands in order to devote themselves
to preaching the Good News. Still others could not survive hours
without reading a fragment from the Bible. They made contests,
offering prizes to anyone who will meet them without the Bible.
The others poured countless amounts of tears, interceding for the
unsaved, calling for the fire of revival in their countries. There were
also those who travelled on a donkey thousands of miles, preaching
the gospel wherever they went.

When I think about these people, I see in them a certain feature:
the hunger to know God, the constant desire for something more. Their lives
were not a matter of a series of accidents. The fact that they gave
themselves to Jesus and sacrificed to serve Him was not an accident. It
was not also the result of unusual or exceptional systematic discipline
as some would say.

They really wanted new things. They did not agree with normality, lukewarmness and mediocrity. They did not agree to stereotypes and overthrow those in whom they did not find God. They pushed ahead, leaving everything to meet the Master, to collide with His power and glory, to know His closeness, sweetness and love – to discover His beauty, His touch and taste. Not looking for their own glory, but God's glory .

Today, when we think about what Luther or John Wesley learned, we wonder what did they learn that through them God brought revival wherever they went. We wonder sometimes how is it possible that so wonderful things had been done, when their doctrines were so imperfect. But everything has its time, and God is not the God of one scheme.

Sometimes it is hard to understand, but that is the way God is. He does not love us because of the perfection of our views. None of us is perfect. The Bible says that our knowledge is in part and our prophesying is in part. God's visitation does not come in response to the perfection of views, but it is a response to our desire. For God the thing that counts the most is the desire to know Him and to be with Him. This is what they had and carried within themselves. They do not agree with the norms or accept the existing state; they searched for and desired something more. The penetrating hunger to know God present in people is a priceless value that makes them go beyond all else.

The Father does not choose only those who meet some specific conditions, so they might know Him. All He expects is hidden in the desire to know Him - the desire of the heart. There has never been and will never be a person who despite fervent and constant hunger in his heart would leave this world unsatisfied, without having met God. Jesus always replies to the genuine cry of the heart. He does not pass over anyone. He does not look at our social status, personality or temperament. He does not require perfection. All He wants is a heart that cries in humility, "Come, my beloved Lord, and let me know You."

God knows our hearts, desires, motives and ambitions. He sees everything and is extremely sensitive. But the Lord wants our whole heart, because always when we come to get more of Him, we have to give more from ourselves. Indeed, the fact we have to give is nothing uncomfortable or difficult.

Often when teens are told that they have to do something, they automatically respond: "If I have to, I'll do everything possible not to do it." Such is religion. So runs the well-known effect of the forbidden fruit. And such is also sin, which gets its stimulus by a set of rules, dos and don'ts. But with God it is totally different, because He is our friend. That we need to do something does not mean that it will be difficult. The effect and fruits count more than the fact of our sacrifice. We can be sure that the fruits will be always greater than our sacrifice.

Many Christians adopt an attitude in life of an ever continuous battle and struggle with God. They have to go to church. They need to pray. They need to look nice. They need to be Christians. This attitude results from the lack of revelation about the immensity of God' love.

That is why I need to meet with God, to collide with His presence, to know Him as someone real. When God comes and meets the needs of our hearts these are beautiful moments. Then all the problems cease to exist. We no longer feel burden but pleasure. There is no battle and in its place a desire appears.

One of my favorite stories in the Bible is the story of Zacchaeus.

> *Then Jesus entered and passed through Jericho. Now behold, there was a man named Zacchaeus who was a chief tax collector, and he was rich. And he sought to see who Jesus was, but could not because of the crowd, for he was of short stature. So he ran ahead and climbed up into a sycamore tree to see Him, for He was going to pass that way. And when Jesus came to the place, He looked up and saw him, and said to him, "Zacchaeus, make haste and come down, for today I must stay at your house." So he made haste and came down, and received Him joyfully. But when they saw it, they all*

complained, saying, "He has gone to be a guest with a man who is a sinner." (Luke 19:1-7, NKJV).

Although I am not a man of small stature, I can wholly identify with Zacchaeus. Why? The reason for that is that I also wanted to see Jesus, know Him and meet with Him. It is a symbol rather than a story about height.

Every one of us in order to meet with God must overcome circumstances, must deal with them, must find his tree. Zacchaeus, despite the fact that he was a highly respected man, did something very silly. He climbed up a tree! Thus he overcame his circumstances.

When the Bible tells us the story of a wealthy, sober and influential man, you seriously imagine a middle-aged, gallant, charismatic and aloof man. Today it could be someone holding a high office, dressed in a fancy suit. Would someone like that jump a tree? But Zacchaeus did!

Sometimes on the way to knowing God we must dare to do strange and difficult things: lose our face, compromise ourselves or do something mad. However, nothing is too high a price to pay on the way to get to knowing Jesus. Nothing.

We have to be ready for this when we decide to seek God. Very soon we will start to hear *grumbling and accusing*. This was the case with Zacchaeus. We will hear strange things from the mouths of people. Accusations, laughter and doubts. This will mean that we are going in the right direction. For God, the most important thing is not our perfection, but our closeness. When Zacchaeus met Jesus, he was a sinful man and the people very quickly pointed it out to him. But our God is a God of love and forgiveness.

For people, of course, our weaknesses and imperfections are what count. For God the most important thing is our presence. He receives each one of us, regardless of our imperfections, and does it with great joy. How wonderful and great news that is!

God revealed it to me when I called to Him to show me my sin. Today I know that perfection is not piety or the correctness. Perfection is knowledge of God's love – it is the presence of God in us. Whenever it is lacking, whenever we leave something for ourselves, the absence of holiness arises. So we can live a perfect life, while not being perfect.

When we do not understand that, it is easy for us to judge others in terms of sinners. A certain passage from the Bible illustrates this very well:

> "But what do you think? A man had two sons, and he came to the first and said, 'Son, go, work today in my vineyard.' He answered and said, 'I will not,' but afterward he regretted it and went. Then he came to the second and said likewise. And he answered and said, 'I go, sir,' but he did not go. Which of the two did the will of his father?" They said to Him, "The first." Jesus said to them, "Assuredly, I say to you that tax collectors and harlots enter the kingdom of God before you. For John came to you in the way of righteousness, and you did not believe him; but tax collectors and harlots believed him; and when you saw it, you did not afterward relent and believe him. (Matthew 21:28–32, NKVJ).

The above fragment reflects Jesus' attitude toward sin. Everyone is a sinner. There is no one in this world without sin. When people brought the adulteress woman to Jesus, He said: *If anyone of you is without sin, let him be the first to throw a stone at her* (John 8:7, NIV). There was not one. Absolutely no one. Also today you will not find anyone.

Once we understand how Jesus sees things, our picture of people, but also ourselves completely changes. God gives us time. He does not require perfection at once. People require it, but not God. That is the difference.

It is very important that when someone says, "So what that you are hungry for God – you still have not dealt with this or that thing". Then you can say with complete freedom: "My God values my closeness more than my immediate perfection"[4]

The second, equally important issue is our motivation. Sometimes we can say one thing, but then we change our mind and we do something else. God values not only our actions and achievements, but most of all the motivations and intentions that inspire them.

Expressing an opinion about something, we are often met with criticism. This applies to all of us. That's the way people are. That's the way are we. God does not judge us, however, on the basis of our desires or errors, but on the basis of the changes taking place in our hearts. When we do wrong, people see that and condemn us. But after some time, we evolve and our perception of some issue changes and it becomes consistent with God's will. It is more valuable for God – a heart ready for molding, evolving and forming. The above passage does not specify the period about which Jesus spoke. It is written that the second man thought it through and then[5] did it.

The Lord has a different view of time. He is patient, understanding and merciful. He does not require immediate perfection.

When I was a teenager and I started to seek God, I did not understand this yet, so it was not so easy. But my desire to know the Lord was greater than any fear!

As a seventeen-year old boy I was baptized in water, and on the eve of the water baptism God baptized me in the Spirit, giving me a new language. From that moment on my desire to know God began to deepen. I knew that this experience could not be the end of my chasing after God. So I prayed for more.

A year after baptism in the Spirit, I found myself in the same room where people prayed for the baptism of the Spirit for me. This time I was there alone. It was then that I experienced for the first time not only God's presence - on that day I met with God. This experience was stronger than the baptism in the Holy Spirit. Then

---

4   In the chapter on religion more on imperfections will be discussed. Imperfection and sin are two different issues. We must not confuse sin with imperfection and treat them synonymously.

5   Hysteros – a Greek word refers to both short and long period - blueletterbible.org

I was filled with one hundred percent certainty that God is there in the room. I felt Him. I heard Him. I met Him.

In Genesis 2 we find a beautiful picture of Moses meeting God.

> Now Moses was tending the flock of Jethro his father-in-law, the priest of Midian. And he led the flock to the back of the desert, and came to Horeb, the mountain of God. And the Angel of the LORD appeared to him in a flame of fire from the midst of a bush. So he looked, and behold, the bush was burning with fire, but the bush was not consumed. Then Moses said, "I will now turn aside and see this great sight, why the bush does not burn." So when the LORD saw that he turned aside to look, God called to him from the midst of the bush and said, "Moses, Moses!"
>
> And he said, "Here I am."
>
> Then He said, "Do not draw near this place. Take your sandals off your feet, for the place where you stand is holy ground." Moreover He said, "I am the God of your father— the God of Abraham, the God of Isaac, and the God of Jacob." And Moses hid his face, for he was afraid to look upon God. (Exodus 3:1-6, NKJV)

An encounter with God is more than simple feeling God's presence. This is a conversation with God, in which He reveals to us His love, holiness and supernatural power. He speaks to us. This is the time when we ask God a question and get an immediate answer. This is the time when we enter God's dimension of holiness.

During an encounter with the Lord we also experience the fear of God. It is not fear, but a clash of human imperfection with the power and holiness of God. We are not overwhelmed with destructive fear, but the feeling of respect, admiration and awareness of the power of God's majesty.

I believe the burning bush was a herald of the coming of the Holy

Spirit's fire. Jesus said He will baptize us with the Holy Spirit and with fire. We should not limit our spiritual life to one experience with Him. The Holy Spirit, our friend, wants more and more for us. With each day and each prayer He wants for us to know Him better and better – that we may burn but not burn out. Moses called it a "great sight". And such "greatness" the Lord desires for each of us.

Later in the story of Moses, we can see what happened after his meeting with the Lord on Mount Sinai. When Moses came down from the mountain and saw the golden calf the people had made, he did not say a word, but immediately burned the calf, ground it to powder and threw it into the water. This is a picture showing how great is the gap between God's holiness and human effort toward our sanctification. When we meet God, we receive the full picture of God's holiness. Knowing God means knowing His holiness. Looking at many of the Puritans, who set for themselves the highest goal to "sanctify" themselves in every aspect of their life, I notice the following relation: continuous pursuit for holiness does not guarantee us the knowledge of God, but an encounter with Him guarantees us knowledge of true holiness.

An encounter with God occurs when at the end of our prayer, we are sure that what we were talking with Him. We are a hundred percent convinced He was talking to us. We are sure of His voice, feelings, love and touch. We get countless instructions concerning what is God's will for our lives. When we "collide" with God, we literally enter into a little piece of heaven - a place where there is nothing but God's presence.

God said to Moses an interesting thing: *Take your sandals off your feet, for the place where you stand is holy ground* (Exodus 3,5, NKJV). We can learn from this story an amazing lesson. When we encounter God we enter holy ground. In that place there is exactly the same atmosphere as in heaven. So we enter into the reality of heaven!

If you want to meet with God, you have to part with your ways of life and your paths. We have to say goodbye to all the worldly ways of thinking, your image of God, your plans, ambitions and methods of operation. God has for us holiness: something completely new, spotless, perfect and beautiful. Something that can't have anything to do with the contamination and dirt of this physical world.

The Holy Scriptures give us many examples of encounters with God in both the Old and New Testament. In Isaiah we read:

> In the year that King Uzziah died, [in a vision] I saw the Lord sitting upon a throne, high and lifted up, and the skirts of His train filled the [most holy part of the] temple. Above Him stood the seraphim; each had six wings: with two [each] covered his [own] face, and with two [each] covered his feet, and with two [each] flew. And one cried to another and said, Holy, holy, holy is the Lord of hosts; the whole earth is full of His glory!

> And the foundations of the thresholds shook at the voice of him who cried, and the house was filled with smoke.

> Then said I, Woe is me! For I am undone and ruined, because I am a man of unclean lips, and I dwell in the midst of a people of unclean lips; for my eyes have seen the King, the Lord of hosts! Then flew one of the seraphim [heavenly beings] to me, having a live coal in his hand which he had taken with tongs from off the altar;

> And with it he touched my mouth and said, Behold, this has touched your lips; your iniquity and guilt are taken away, and your sin is completely atoned for and forgiven.

> Also I heard the voice of the Lord, saying, Whom shall I send? And who will go for Us? Then said I, Here am I; send me. (Isaiah 6:1-8, AMP)

An encounter with God is a time of intense experiences. Both spiritual and physical. You cannot meet God, pray and remain the same. Every encounter with God brings changes into your life – a change of perspective in viewing the world and our hearts. It brings forth a hunger and thirst for something more.

In each encounter with Jesus, there are a few important elements. The first is awareness of God's holiness and power. We cannot meet God, suspecting that there is in Him even a tiny bit of imperfection. God is perfect and holy in His love. The second element is the clash of God's holiness with human imperfection. In a moment we realize how imperfect and dirt we are. The third element is the love of God. God always shows us that despite our dirt He loves us, forgives us and longs for our presence. Back in the Old Testament Isaiah's vision was the prophetic picture of God's redemptive plan of salvation.

Next to the last element of an encounter with God is conversation with Him. We speak to God and He speaks to us. The final element is the fruit of this conversation - the manifesting presence of God.

Every encounter with Him will carry within itself something significant – the glory we see, the power that God allows us to know, the voice we hear. You will want to return to this place and get to know God closer.

The same elements can be seen in the history of Saul, the apostle.

> *As he was traveling, it happened that he was approaching Damascus, and suddenly a light from heaven flashed around him; and he fell to the ground and heard a voice saying to him, "Saul, Saul, why are you persecuting Me?" And he said, "Who are You, Lord?" And He said, "I am Jesus whom you are persecuting, but get up and enter the city, and it will be told you what you must do." The men who traveled with him stood speechless, hearing the [c]voice but seeing no one. Saul got up from the ground, and though his eyes were open, he [d]could see nothing; and leading him by the hand, they brought him into Damascus. And he was three days without sight, and neither ate nor drank. (Acts 9:3-9, NASB)*

The beautiful thing about the history of Saul is that the light blinded him but not the others. They all heard the thunder but they did not hear the voice. They saw the light but did not see the person. From the Greek point of view it is not logical. But Jesus did not deal with us according to Greek logic. He communicates with people at the level of the heart. He does it individually and personally, although He often speaks to the whole crowd.

I remember some of these encounters with God, like when I sat, just as any other week in the church pew. Nothing special was happening. The service was the same as usual. Nothing stood out in any way. But it was during these normal services God came down to me in His glory with such power that I could not stop crying or get up from the floor. I fell to my knees and couldn't get up. The Holy Spirit spoke to me, washing away all the cares, worries and doubts. Another time, the presence of God was so strong that I had to literally run away from the meeting, because I knew I would not be able to stand on my feet and that strange things would start to happen with my body.

The thing that distinguishes our times from the times of the Old Testament is that back then God spoke and revealed Himself only to the prophets, kings and priests. Today, thanks to the blood of the Lamb, absolutely everyone can benefit from grace and enter into the Holy of Holies, the place of God's glory. This is wonderful, good news for everyone!

What moves me the most in the story of Paul is the permanence of his experience. When God meets with us, we will never be the same again. Never. Reading the book of Acts we can see in later chapters what was Jesus' mission for Paul. He did not meet with Paul so that the apostle would only keep the experience for himself. The desire of Jesus was, and still is, to talk about Him! The first and ultimate goal of Paul's mission was Jesus Christ Himself.

Certainly, Jesus instruct us to preach the good news, and he never said that we should use words when necessary. This is one of those beautiful false statements that allows us to have spiritual apathy and change our true mission into religion.[6]

Today it is extremely sad that encounters with God seem to be reserved only for some individuals. Many wonderful treasures and spiritual pearls are lost because of the label of false modesty. Speaking about God always kindles a hunger in one's heart. So we need to get out of the closet and talk about God: about His great wonders, about His beauty, love and immense glory.

The Apostle Paul did not keep what he experienced only for himself. It was not Jesus' intention. On the contrary, Jesus wanted that the whole world would know about it! On the next few occasions Paul talked about it both to Jews and top government officials, with king Agrippa at the head. God wants it today: that the whole world may know that He is real and alive.

When I think about all the people from the Bible who met the Lord, I can see one fundamental thing. It did not happen because of their holiness but it was always the result of their deep desire and not agreeing for what they already had. Moses killed the Egyptian. Saul persecuted Christians in the name of faith. Isaiah was broken because of Israel's sin and apostasy. All of them were full of passion and fervor. They burned with unquenchable hunger. They lived with constant chasing, not settling with normality. They wanted something more. This is the only way to meet the Lord – having a desperate and hungry heart.

When God met me the first time, I was teenager. Now I know that God is a real person, and every encounter with Him has always been and will be unique.

Without meeting with God we will never be able to tell others the difference between a divine touch and God's glory or God's presence and the power of God. The key to today's Christianity is an encounter with God. This key opens the door to a new dimension of Christian life.

---

[6]   Of course, this is not a rule. Sometimes our life says more than words. It all depends on the circumstances and time, but I believe very strongly that this statement chase the initiative away from the Church, changing the gospel into law.

We may limit ourselves to theory. We may put Christianity on the shelf along with other interests and philosophies. We can also begin a daily life full of excitement and new discoveries in the wonder of God's glory.

An encounter with God is the time when everything from earth loses its charm and splendor, and becomes completely devoid of meaning. The problems of the world no longer make any impression on us.

When we are aware of God as a person and we know that the flesh and the earth we are living on is only a short episode in eternity, our life takes on a different dimension. We stop focusing on problems. We start focusing on Him.

This is what the Lord craves for in all of us. He wants to meet us, He wants us to know Him and to live a life full of unforgettable encounters with Him.

In the next chapter we will talk about the feelings of the Father. We will also answer the question of whether Jesus has the same feelings as a man and can Father God show the same love as our earthly father. We will also explain how strong God's feelings may be and how do they differ from human feelings and emotions.

Prayer

(Lyrics: Jesus meet me, Marc James)

Filthy with my sin I come to you
Nothing left to bring, I cry out to You
From all these worthless things I turn to You
In my barrenness I worship You

chor. Jesus meet me, come Lord save
Wash me clean and make me holy
I was born to love You only
Spirit come breath your life within me

STUDY QUESTIONS

➢ What distinguishes men of God? What is their common feature?

➢ Are you ready for the same sacrifice as Zacchaeus dared to give in order to meet the Lord?

➢ Jesus said He will baptize us in the Holy Spirit and in fire. Do you think you were baptized in fire?

➢ Thanks to what we can benefit from grace and enter into the Holy of Holies?

➢ Have you already met with God? Do you want to encounter God and know Him in person?

O God, You *are* my God;
Early will I seek You;
My soul thirsts for You;
My flesh longs for You
In a dry and thirsty land
Where there is no water.
So I have looked for You in the sanctuary,
To see Your power and Your glory.
Because Your lovingkindness *is* better than life,
My lips shall praise You.
Thus I will bless You while I live;
I will lift up my hands in Your name.
My soul shall be satisfied as with marrow and fatness,
And my mouth shall praise *You* with joyful lips.
When I remember You on my bed,
I meditate on You in the *night* watches.
Because You have been my help,
Therefore in the shadow of Your wings I will rejoice.
My soul follows close behind You;
Your right hand upholds me.
(Psalm 63,1–8, *NKJV*)

4

HOLY EMOTIONS

Religion strips the Church today from what is
most beautiful: holy feelings of God Himself;
it places mankind higher than his Creator.

I f my heaven would run out of emotion, it would not be heaven.
Emotions are an integral part of life with God and just as
important and natural as in human relations.

It makes me wonder why so many believers perceive emotionalism
as a negative phenomenon. Why is the importance of emotions and
feelings pushed to the side so often? Why does the church run away
from emotions and fear emotionalism? If feelings in our family
relations were lacking, it would be hard to find the purpose of life.
We wouldn't be able to learn from each other through copying
each other's behavior. We wouldn't be able to react, to know or
to experience. Everything would be colorless, boring, gray and
indifferent.

When God created man, He made him in His image and likeness.
There was nothing about depriving mankind of feelings because He
had feelings Himself.

In psychology, feelings are considered to be a direct stimulus for
emotions. Without feelings there would be no emotions. Feelings

would only be cherished and unexpressed attitudes if it wasn't for emotions. The world would be emotionless.

It is hard for me to think of a mother holding her newborn child for the first time and feeling no excitement at all or a father with a stone face listening to his son talking about how he just got engaged. There are thousands of such instances: college exams, newlyweds longing for their wedding night or a call from the hospital informing parents about the health of their child …

I remember my mom telling me what she had experienced when they called her from the hospital and asked: "Hello, I'm calling from the hospital. Am I speaking with Marcin's mother?". This shock was hard to describe. My mom said that she was expecting anything at that moment. Thoughts and questions seemed to rush endlessly through her mind. Fortunately, it turned out the call was "only" concerning broken hands.

If we were emotionless, life would be meaningless. Nothing would matter to us. This raises the question: Am I not to respond with emotions concerning what the Holy Spirit does for me? Shouldn't I be happy, jump, dance, shout and cry?

Lots of emotions have occurred in my life ever since I started to look for God. They became an integral part of my life with God. I was excited many times whenever I thought about what I will be doing during my conversation with God at night. I was impatiently waiting for everyone to go to sleep so that I could spend time with the Lord again. I loved those all-night moments spent with my most wonderful friend.

It's just like with lovers who all the time think about what they will say or ask the other when they will meet their partner again. One can fall in love with Jesus as well and it can be accompanied by many emotions. There is nothing wrong with expressing our emotions.

While studying various Bible translations a few years ago I realized that there is a certain expression which appears in Corinthians and which perfectly captures the sense of what I experience.

And my language and my message were not set forth in persuasive (enticing and plausible) words of wisdom, but they were in demonstration of the [Holy] Spirit and power [a proof by the Spirit and power of God, operating on me and stirring in the minds of my hearers the most holy emotions and thus persuading them], so that your faith might not rest in the wisdom of men (human philosophy), but in the power of God. (1 Corinthians 2:4-5; AMP).

I love this phrase! The Holy Spirit stirs in me holy emotions! I felt them and I still feel them to this day. This passage shows us that human emotions and holy emotions exist. Sadness, joy, laughter and tears are caused by human sensitivity but there are also emotions arising apart from my feelings. These are emotions born as a result of a relationship with the Holy Spirit.

A certain event is worth mentioning here of which, I think, will clearly convey the picture. I was listening to a song from the movie "Into the Wild" once. I decided to listen to it again so I pressed the appropriate button. Immediately I started to cry. My brother who was busy with his own stuff heard this song as well and also started to cry. I didn't know this because I was in another room at that time. This went on for maybe two hours. The Holy Spirit was doing something in us. He was washing, cleansing, changing and inspiring us.

I've often wondered whether all these strange feelings, which appeared in me quite suddenly and without any reasonable connection to what actually had happened, originated within me, were made up by me, were a twist of fate or a figment of my imagination. I also wondered if they could come from an improper source.

I also remember a special moment. I came to my church to pray in the evening as usual. It was a very intense time in my life. I was not granted a visa to the United States, which made me dismayed and sad. I waited several years for that special day when I could fly to Tampa, Florida and meet the pastor who greatly influenced my life. I experienced some difficult moments on my way back from the US embassy in Krakow. There were tears, disappointment and sadness. The period of my life that I had planned for the opening of a new chapter, was crossed off in a single moment. All hope left and only emptiness remained.

I returned to my home and later started to plan to go to church as soon as possible. I wanted to talk it over with my Daddy. I longed for it because I knew that everything would become clear. The Holy Spirit would tell me why this happened and what to do next. I turned on the music and began to pray or rather cry out to God.

A number of wonderful things that are difficult to describe happened during that time of prayer. My heart was filled with sadness while I simultaneously waited on what God would tell me. I cried, but I also knew that He has everything in His hands and that it all makes sense.

And that's when God came to me with emotions I never knew before. I fell to the ground after few minutes of prayer. I got up after a while which seemed to me to be a natural behavior, yet I fell down again after few seconds. Eventually, I bravely stood up again. At that moment bizarre things started to happen with my body. I was absolutely sure it was the Holy Spirit. I let the Lord work in me and touch me.

God's powerful presence visited me in that place and the intensity of the emotions was extremely strong. My heart was beating hard and fast.

I was crying uncontrollably and then started to laugh after a minute. All this was accompanied by an enormous peace and love. And right then, in the midst of extraordinary emotions, I felt like God was saying: "Your ways are not My ways, and My thoughts are not your thoughts".

Instantly, I realized that I did the planning of my future over the last few years instead of God. It was all my idea. Although it was good, God was not in it. The Holy Spirit wanted to teach me one simple lesson: *He wants us to ask Him what His will is.* If we know His will, we will never blame Him because we will know the difference between His ways and ours.

Often we hold a grudge against God, yet the problem lies in the fact that we do not talk with Him and we do not know what *His* plans are. After my prayer God filled me with a blissful peace. I knew that His thoughts are good and that there was nothing to worry about. Although I was sad in my heart, I knew that the Lord would take care of my future. I was sure of it. I trusted Jesus.

Today, being filled by the peace of God, I know the Holy Spirit shapes and makes emotions to stimulate us into a relationship with Him. The Holy Spirit convinces us so that our faith will be based on the power of God rather than human philosophy[7].

We need such experiences to bind us with God, to make us remember certain events as special and to remember the exact course of certain prayers – we know what happened at that time and what its purpose was.

During those dramatic experiences the most important thing was that nobody prepared me for it and I had never heard of something like this happening before. But when the Lord came, I simply yielded to all He was doing. Without a shadow of a doubt I knew it was Him.

It's hard to long for God if our spiritual life is stripped of feelings and relationship with Him. Our thinking about marriage or first love is accompanied by a vastness of feelings. Very often we remember certain meetings due to emotions and feelings that accompanied those special moments. The same is with God. It is very difficult to long if there are no emotions in our past, which we could cherish, or if there are no moments of particular value to us. After all, it is the longing that brings us closer to God and deepens our love.

Emotions also have a *purpose*. The Bible teaches it clearly. The term "trance" appears in the Scriptures (KJV) three times. It is defined as: "a throwing of the mind out of its normal state, alienation of mind manifested by a sudden surge of emotion or turning off the mind. Although the person is awake, his mind is drawn off and wholly fixed on the things of God (…)"[8].

---

7   More on the power of God in chapter ten.

8   blueletterbible.org, number 1611 in Strong's concordance.

Moreover, the term "being in the spirit" repeatedly occurs in the Bible. Also the important thing here is for our mind to be turned off so that the spirit could be free. It is difficult to understand when we perceive relationship with God as a human philosophy[9]. However, our concept of relationship with God changes completely when we believe that God is spirit and we were made in His image and likeness.

I believe in the Word of God. I believe in the God of the Bible. That is why I also believe that what the apostles experienced in the past is available for the Church today.

Each time the term *trance* or *being in the spirit* appeared in the Bible it was for a specific purpose. The Apostle Peter received a vision and John received the Word of Revelation. There is always a reason when God comes down to us. It is impossible for our body not to feel excitement in moments like that. It is actually the opposite. Our body feels emotions difficult to bear[10].

Psalm 63 says:

> *O God, You are my God; I shall seek You earnestly; My soul thirsts for You, my flesh yearns for You, in a dry and weary land where there is no water. (Psalm 63:1, NASB)*

David in the Old Testament was able to distinguish the sphere of the body from the spirit. He did not say: *I long for You*, but expressed himself more precisely: *my flesh (body) longs for you*. David longed for a physical touch and that's what he talked to God about. Perhaps it is a difficult subject and only a few have the courage to talk about it, however, emotions are very often mentioned in the Scriptures. This is not a secondary subject for me. I cannot imagine life with God without feelings or excitement about His wonderful person.

Without emotions, life with God would look like the life of a person in a relationship with another person who lacks empathy and

---

[9]   For certain Christianity and God's kingdom have their own philosophy and ideology, but it has nothing to do with man's limited humanism.

[10]   More on the inadequacies of the body in chapter eleven.

understanding. I find it hard to even think about a situation in which there is a marriage problem but it is ignored because a spouse shows *no* interest whatsoever.

We do not feel good when we are ignored. Mutual acceptance, understanding, conversation and help are the main purposes of marriage. Our life with God is similar. I cannot remain indifferent when God speaks to me. I cannot show a lack of interest when He touches me. I would certainly grieve my Lord if I did so.

The complete elimination of emotions from the life of the Church makes God only an object of our philosophy. Relationship with God becomes limited to faith based on human wisdom. If I was to believe in God who I was told about but did not get to know Him personally, and my faith was to be based on human wisdom, I suspect I'd be easily convinced to accept the doctrine of the Jehovah's Witnesses or some *humanist interpretation* of the Bible. But my faith is not based on human wisdom or the doctrine of the Church. It is based on the power and person of God[11].

In the Bible we can also read about trembling that accompanied people who met with the Lord.

> *But Jesus said, "Somebody touched Me, for I perceived power going out from Me." Now when the woman saw that she was not hidden, she came trembling; and falling down before Him, she declared to Him in the presence of all the people the reason she had touched Him and how she was healed immediately. And He said to her, "Daughter, be of good cheer; your faith has made you well. Go in peace."* (Luke 8: 46-48, NKJV).

---

[11] Of course no one is attempting to ignore the authority of the Word here. The Bible says that Jesus is the Word. However, the word can be the letter and the Word can also be the revelation of the Person of Jesus. These two are entirely opposite concepts. The Word of God always is and will be the revelation of the person, whereas it will never negate it.

When I think about it, I see an image of a woman filled with incredible emotions before meeting with Jesus. Her pounding heart is filled with love. She is not afraid, yet trembling. Her body is shaking with emotion. She is all shook up for in just a moment she will meet the Lord Himself face to face.

One cannot remain indifferent when meeting God. It is impossible not to feel emotions since they are an essential element in our relationship with Him.

There is one difference between emotions that are from God and from man: God's emotions are always positive. There are many negative emotions that arise in our lives due anger, hurt, betrayal, violence, slander, etc. In our relationship with God, such emotions never occur. God is good and full of love. All that He does is motivated by love and for our well-being. This is why emotions from God differ from man's emotions. Therefore, everything we experience with God is good and all emotions coming from God are positive.

Religion robs the Church today from that which is the most beautiful: the holy feelings of God Himself. It places man higher than his Creator. Religion destroys the image of God as a Person and blocks the way of the Holy Spirit to express *His* emotions in us. This is mostly due to an ambiguous approach to strange situations that have taken place in some charismatic circles. For example, during the spiritual outpouring in Toronto people talked about demonic manifestations. Similar opinions are expressed about Kansas City or laughter in the Spirit. There are many allegations and the Internet is full of accusations in relation to behaviors of this kind.

The Book of Ezra in the Old Testament describes a prayer meeting that perfectly illustrates God's model of diversity in the Church.

> *When the builders laid the foundation of the temple of the* LORD, *the priests stood in their apparel with trumpets, and the Levites, the sons of Asaph, with cymbals, to praise the* LORD, *according to the*

ordinance of David king of Israel. And they sang responsively, praising and giving thanks to the LORD:

"For He is good, For His mercy endures forever toward Israel." Then all the people shouted with a great shout, when they praised the LORD, because the foundation of the house of the LORD was laid.

But many of the priests and Levites and heads of the fathers' houses, old men who had seen the first temple, wept with a loud voice when the foundation of this temple was laid before their eyes. Yet many shouted aloud for joy, so that the people could not discern the noise of the shout of joy from the noise of the weeping of the people, for the people shouted with a loud shout, and the sound was heard afar off. (Ezra. 3:10-13, NKJV)

Many Christians do not make room for diversity in the Church. However, we must understand that everyone is different. The Church would make no sense if God created us identical. People also create diversity. Each one of us is orginal and special. All of us are a part of a local church and helps form its character.

One of the reasons for this is the difference of opinions between the older and younger generations. God is showing us in His Word that generational differences should not be a problem but a tool to create power in unity. The aforementioned passage shows the harmony and unity of the Church despite diversity.

The situation described in the Book of Ezra shows that it was not only a difference of opinion but the extreme difference in the way of expressing admiration and praise. When the Holy Spirit comes to us with His presence we react differently, although the purpose may be the same. Both groups were filled with great joy back then, only the form of expression was different. However, it did not hinder the common exaltation of God. The effects were apparently surprising.

We must not forget one important thing when discussing

emotionality. In 2 Corinthians the Apostle Paul gives us an exact answer as to what our attitude toward emotions should be.

> *(...) so that you can answer those who take pride in what is seen rather than in what is in the heart. If we are "out of our mind," as some say, it is for God; if we are in our right mind, it is for you. For Christ's love compels us (...)*
> (2 Cor. 5: 12-14; NIV)

This passage actually answers every question about emotions. If we are insane, it is not for men but to God. It is very easy to distinguish. When the Holy Spirit comes, we begin to feel emotions and our body responds to Him. However, it shouldn't be the reason for boasting among the people – this happens for us only and we have to *save* it in our spiritual portfolio. This results from the fact that it will be extremely difficult for us to describe it or explain to others.

There are several passages in the Scriptures that also talk about manifestations of the Holy Spirit. Samson, overwhelmed by the Spirit, performed mighty deeds in the power of God. We also read that the Holy Spirit came *powerfully* on Saul and *he was changed into a different person* (NIV). We cannot act normally when something similar is happening to us. When the Holy Spirit overwhelms us, He takes over our emotions and will. We are completely subjected to Him during these few "overwhelming" moments. That is also when He does whatever He desires. The New Testament calls it the "anointing".

Churches nowadays experience many mystifications and imitations of the Holy Spirit. Hence, I think, such restraint toward emotional issues. But nowhere in His Word did God say that He wants to limit our relationship with Him to a bond devoid of emotion. On the contrary, He left us some instructions. He does not come so that we would boast about the outward appearance. He always comes for a specific purpose and our role is to give Him all the glory.

The aforementioned passage is also the answer for all the opponents of emotion. It stresses the great and special intimacy Jesus shares with man. This is the answer to every question relating to emotion. It is something personal between Him, and us regardless of what is happening in our lives and our relationship with God. Intimacy with Him is the answer to every allegation, doubt and accusation in this respect[12].

When our personal lives with God experience a myriad of different emotions and experiences, the stories of suspicious "incidents" in churches do not surprise us. It all becomes normal to us. Explaining the authenticity and origin of such behaviors is not in our power since these emotions do not belong to us.

I am not a supporter of excessive emotionality emphasized in the church in any case. I will never approve an attitude that says, "The more manifestations of a physical touch of the Lord in my life, the closer I am to the Lord". There are many imitations of a true touch of the Lord. It happens very often but it is natural and results from the lack of intimacy with God. Those who know and cherish the presence of the Holy Spirit in their lives will never attempt to imitate His touch.

On the other hand I am not a supporter of removing emotions from the church because it would be as though we would have said to God: "Good Lord, you can work but don't overdo it!". The Lord desires relationship based on freedom, passion and trust rather than lifeless conservatism.

In conclusion, we can state that the human heart is the only verifying factor for the authenticity of experience with God. The truth lies deep only in the human heart. If someone approaches me and tries to convince me that the things that took place are "wrong and do not fit me" because they are "inappropriate emotions", my heart will be at peace because I'll be confident that it came from the Lord - my beloved Friend. I will know their source and the place they were born.

---

[12]   I think that due to this passage of the Scripture many different manifestations of a physical touch are reserved for our personal time with the Lord unless they happen in unity and as a result of the outpouring of the Holy Spirit on everyone - as it was at the Pentecost. If we manifest it in public, we behave like a married couple who show in public things that are reserved for them only.

Let us remember we need balance in all aspects of Christianity. Extremes will never lead to peace but rather to splits and unnecessary strife that often ends in divisions, unforgiveness or trauma.

If we want to go one step further in our relationship with the Lord, we will also have to deal with the greatest enemy of freedom - fear. First of all - fear of the unknown and secondly - fear of accusations. We won't be truly free in our relationship with Jesus as long as we hold on to it.

The next chapter will deal with fear. In fact, anxiety is a threat that powerfully paralyzes and limits our path to a relationship with the Lord – a relationship based on complete freedom – closing the door to a new dimension of an intimate and exciting friendship.

Prayer

(Lyrics: Hillsong, The Stand)

SO WHAT COULD I SAY
WHAT COULD I DO
BUT OFFER THIS HEART, OH GOD
COMPLETELY TO YOU

I'll stand with arms high and heart abandoned
In awe of the One who gave it all I'll stand
My soul Lord to you surrendered,
All I am is Yours

STUDY QUESTIONS

➢ Do you think that all emotions are bad? Are you afraid of emotions? Why?

➢ Did you ever meet with strange manifestations of emotionality? What do you think about it?

➢ Do you think a relationship with God should be devoid of feelings and emotions?

➢ What does the Bible say about the *state of trance*? Do we fall in *state of trance* for the Lord or for the people? Explain.

➢ How does God reveal Himself in each of us? Are there different forms of a touch of God? How do you explain the term *belief in diversity*?

The LORD is my light and my salvation—
whom should I fear?
The LORD is the stronghold of my life—
of whom should I be afraid?
When evildoers came against me to devour my flesh,
my foes and my enemies stumbled and fell.
Though an army deploys against me,
my heart is not afraid;
though a war breaks out against me,
still I am confident.
I have asked one thing from the LORD;
it is what I desire:
to dwell in the house of the LORD
all the days of my life,
gazing on the beauty of the LORD
and seeking Him in His temple.

(Psalm 27:1-4, HCSB)

5
FEAR OF THE UNKNOWN

Fear is one of the greatest tools of the devil. Wherever fear
appears, it causes God to look like He is far away.

I t was a late summer evening. The youth meeting finished two
hours ago. Everyone else was already gone but a few of us still
stayed to fool around and listen to loud rock music. By midnight,
there were only two of us left. We decided to pray and play Morning
Star's new album "Glory" which was the latest record at the time as
well as a big hit in charismatic circles.

I can still remember today the little plastic computer speakers that
could barely make any sound in not a tiny room. However, it didn't
bother us at all. The most important thing for us was to be able to
hear the melody.

That was the first time the Holy Spirit came upon me with a *river
of living waters,* as the Bible calls it. I sensed the presence of God in my
body. I was lying down on the floor, listening to the beautiful music
coming out from the speakers. I was praying in the Holy Spirit when
suddenly I started to feel a strange shiver in my belly that I never had
before. Yes! It certainly was the Holy Spirit!

Now, I know, but back then I had doubts. The enemy came
trying to do everything possible to scare me with anxiety, fear and
doubts. I had no idea what the Bible said about this at that time.

It is difficult to talk about things like that because experiences with an element of physical manifestation of the Spirit are often treated with detachment and leniency, whereas in some circles they are firmly condemned and called deception.

But as for us believers, we need to not only hear about the God of the letter of the law and seriousness, but also about God whose presence goes beyond understanding of the human mind - about the God of love and power. Many people wonder whether God can also be felt in a physical way. I remember once somebody asked me, "When you pray several hours do some cool things happen?". Hearing this I smiled to myself and answered vaguely because in our relationship with God, building a foundation of love is much more important than physical fruits. I think this sort of issue needs to be clarified, since I was asked the question of whether I think 'can God be physically felt' several times.

The Gospel of John says,

> In the last day, that great day of the feast, Jesus stood and cried, saying, If any man thirst, let him come unto me, and drink. He that believeth on me, as the scripture hath said, out of his belly shall flow rivers of living water.(KJV)
> But this spake he of the Spirit, which they that believe on him should receive: for the Holy Ghost was not yet given; because that Jesus was not yet glorified. (Young's)
> (John 7:37-39).

I was very happy when I heard the Word saying that out of our belly shall flow rivers of living water[13] because I actually felt something in my belly several times. God confirmed that the Holy Spirit comes on us and lets us feel Him in a physical way as well. Before I learned that, however, Satan attacked me constantly with fear of what was unknown to me. But the Bible says: *Perfect love casts out fear* (1 John 4:18, NKJV).

---

[13]   I heard preaching on this subject by pastor Rodney Howard-Browne.

Now I know that love for Jesus is the most important thing we need in life. We need to trust that *whatever* He does in response to the hunger of our hearts comes from Him. You cannot truly pray to the Father for understanding of Himself and receive a stone, snake or scorpion.

In the Gospel of Matthew we read,

> *Keep on asking, and you will receive what you ask for. Keep on seeking, and you will find. Keep on knocking, and the door will be opened to you. For everyone who asks, receives. Everyone who seeks, finds. And to everyone who knocks, the door will be opened. "You parents—if your children ask for a loaf of bread, do you give them a stone instead? Or if they ask for a fish, do you give them a snake? Of course not! So if you sinful people know how to give good gifts to your children, how much more will your heavenly Father give good gifts to those who ask him.* (Matthew 7:7-11, NLT).

If I ask God for bread, I won't receive a stone. If I ask for a fish, I won't receive a snake. If I ask for the Holy Spirit, I won't receive an evil spirit.

Life with God is simple. God is love. There is no fear in love and perfect love casts out all fear[14]. The Bible says our Heavenly Father wants to give us good things. The one and only condition is to ask for them.

We often think that God knows what is good for us and it is highly inappropriate to ask the Lord for new, great and wonderful things. We are told that if there is something He wants to give us, He'll give it to us on His own. However, the Bible does not say that the Father will give good things to those who won the lottery. No. The Bible says that the Father gives to those who seek, knock and ask. *Ask and it shall be given you; seek, and you shall find.* It is a great pleasure for the Father to listen to our requests and give us good things.

---

14   1 John 4:16-18

Impatience and waiting for instant answers is common and typical today. But God does not work that way. He looks for vessels ready for sacrifice and humility. God is not a benefactor distributing good gifts to strangers randomly passing Him at a festival. This is not the way He works. The gifts are given to those who ask, seek and knock.

Asking and seeking are not mere activities but processes in which the Lord examines our hearts, searches us and prepares us. Ask *until* you receive. Seek and *do not stop* – be persistent and patient. Jesus does not expect us to only do the actions of these simple instructions. He wants our hearts. It is something that seems to be the most important at this point. Ask, seek and knock *until* your hearts will be ready to receive. This is what the Father wants to tell us, I believe. He does not want to give us something that we won't use. The Lord gives us what we ask for when we are ready to receive it.

The words: *Do not be afraid* can be found in the Bible over a hundred times[15]. This is the most frequent command given to us by God. God wants to tell us something here. God's desire for His children is for them to live in total freedom from fear because fear is one of the biggest tools of the devil. Wherever fear appears, it causes God to look like He is far away. And this is one of the main goals of the devil today – to make Jesus distant, unreachable and uninterested in the believer's life. That is why God repeated so often the words: *Do not be afraid!*

We can treat this as a constant and universal principle: regardless of what happens in our lives, God says: *Do not be afraid!*. He is with us as a Father. He's there to watch over, care for and protect us. There is no reason for us to be afraid. God is always with us!

When John met Jesus in the first chapter of Revelation, we read: *So when I saw him, I fell at His feet as dead.* What did Jesus answer him? *Fear not, I am the first and the last, and the living. I was dead, and behold I am alive for evermore, and I hold the keys of death and hell.* This is the exact response of Jesus concerning fear. He always answers: *Do not be afraid.*

---

[15] It appears 115 to 155 times depending on the English translation of the Bible. The most authoritative translation, KJV, has this phrase 103 times.

The story of Jesus walking on water reveals another great truth about fear to us:

> *Now in the fourth watch of the night Jesus went to them, walking on the sea. And when the disciples saw Him walking on the sea, they were troubled, saying, "It is a ghost!" And they cried out for fear. But immediately Jesus spoke to them, saying, "Be of good cheer! It is I; do not be afraid. "And Peter answered Him and said, "Lord, if it is You, command me to come to You on the water. "So He said, "Come." And when Peter had come down out of the boat, he walked on the water to go to Jesus. But when he saw that the wind was boisterous, he was afraid; and beginning to sink he cried out, saying, "Lord, save me! "And immediately Jesus stretched out His hand and caught him, and said to him, "O you of little faith, why did you doubt?"* (Matthew 14:25-31, NKJV).

Be of good cheer! It is I! Do not be afraid. These were the first words of Jesus to his disciples during the storm. However, Peter was afraid despite the fact that Jesus spoke these words.

Fear has tremendous power. This story not only shows that even such great apostles like Peter had a problem with fear, but also draws attention to the great power which is embedded in a life free from fear. Freedom from fear opens the way to powerful faith for us. Fear is the direct and main reason for the lack of faith.

Moreover, the story shows us that people have a tendency to concentrate on the circumstances rather than on Jesus. The response to fear is to keep our eyes fixed on Jesus. Keeping our eyes on Jesus we leave no room for fear or doubt in our lives. Instead of looking at Jesus, Peter looked away and saw the terrible condition of the sea that caused him to fear. Today, Jesus wants everyone to know that if we look to him, fear will not have access to us. This is the only solution to fear!

Fear hinders the Holy Spirit from being in full communion with us in our relationship with God. Let me give you an example. My colleague from work got married few years ago. When I asked him how his marriage is going after two years, he said: "Man! I could not even go out for an hour without the phone ringing. But the problem was not my wife who called me. It was both my wife and my mother-in-law who called me! I could not stand it anymore".

Unfortunately, there is no true love without trust. The same is true with God. He desires our trust. There is no need to quote dozens of verses about trust at this point. God tells us: "Trust in Me and I will do it all". And we know that the trust comes when we have time for each other, to learn, know and trust each other.

Several years have passed since my first encounter with the Holy Spirit. Fear is not a problem for me today. I know that whatever God does, He does it for my good. Ever since God revealed to me in His Word that the Holy Spirit does not come only in the form of the wind but also as rain and fire, I know His ways are different. I never try to limit the Holy Spirit in how He wants to manifest Himself because I know that everything has its time and purpose.

Fear is the main reason for many Christians not to experience the presence of the Holy Spirit and hear His voice. This happens because the Holy Spirit often tries to get our attention by external signs when He speaks to us. There are hundreds of such instances in the Bible. When God spoke, heaven thundered and people fell down in trembling because they were overcome by divine power. The Holy Spirit wants us to concentrate on Him. He cannot speak when we are busy thinking about the loan or future events. That is why He often draws our attention through a physical touch. We need to be ready in love to receive Him when He comes, so that He could speak to us, touch and change us.

I started to consider the subject of fear as priority and paid special attention to my own thoughts ever since I sensed Holy Spirit's voice: *Do not be afraid*! It was through other people or during my time of prayer. I searched my heart for even a little bit of fear because there is no situation in which God wants us to be afraid.

In Isaiah, God gives us incredible promise:

I will build you using fairness. You will be safe from those who would hurt you, so you will have nothing to fear. Nothing will come to make you afraid. I will not send anyone to attack you. (Isaiah 54:14–15a, NCV).

We have no reason to be afraid. Never! We can be sure that our Lord is with us to protect us in every situation. This is the attitude God desires for us. Freedom from all fear and terror.

There is a widespread belief in many Christian circles that every believer should *fear the Lord*. The Bible talks about it frequently. However, the *fear of the Lord* does not mean to be *afraid of God*. The fear of the Lord means to be of the same heart as the Lord Jesus. It means to distinguish good from evil and abhor evil.

The Bible says: *The fear of the Lord is to hate evil* (Proverbs 8:13, NKJV). And: *The fear of the Lord is the beginning of knowledge* (Proverbs 1:7 NKJV). Here God explains to us what the fear of the Lord is and what He means by it. His desire and purpose is not to make us afraid of Him and run away from Him. Our Father is not a despotic ruler who chases us each time we stumble or fall. God's desire for us is to fear sin and flee from every form of evil. He wants us to be aware of the consequences of sin and judgment and to know how sad Jesus is when we sin. This is the true fear of God.

The Bible is very clear: *I will never leave you nor forsake you* (Hbr. 13,5, NKJV). And: *For the mountains shall depart and the hills be removed, but My kindness shall not depart from you, nor shall My covenant of peace be removed.* (Is. 54:10, NKJV).

God's love and grace are indisputable. Let us not be fooled, do not be afraid of God.

Another extremely important issue is the fear of accusation. There is a lot to say about this because unless it's clearly understood, it will cause people to face God's judgment very quickly.

Scripture says that the kindness of God leads us to repentance. Satan does everything possible to accuse us and turn our eyes away from Jesus so that we would focus on our sin and guilt. But God wants something completely different. The Lord always wants us to return to His holy and redeeming blood, the power of which cannot be overestimated. The blood of Jesus has the power of eternity within it. There is no greater power of forgiveness than the holy blood of Jesus. The Lord never forbade us to come back to His cross and blood. We can do it anytime and be sure that His blood will always have the same power to cleanse us from all unrighteousness and to make us holy in God's sight.

Accusation is the basic tool of the devil, causing fear in the hearts of Christians. I clearly remember one day when I did everything in my power to make sure every detail was covered in my ministry. It did not prevent a certain man from saying, "Many people resign because of you". I felt a huge blow. Immediately all life left me. The word "discouragement" wouldn't thoroughly convey my spiritual condition. I was not discouraged but bruised and completely wrecked.

I went to my prayer closet, to my heavenly court and told God everything. I screamed, being unable to bear the fact that I did everything I could to organize this event the way it should be and yet people resign because of me. I did not understand it completely.

Then I felt like God speaking to me words that changed my perspective in understanding accusations forever: "Do not be afraid! I never accuse you. Stand on the Word, which, as you know, comes from me".

It was not just a simple sentence. It was something that pierced my entire being. It pierced me as though it was a person. I cried so much. I was laying on the floor overcome by the love of God. I felt as though a sweet spiritual substance filled my whole being. I knew that no accusation would ever again have even the slightest impact on my life. I became completely free from accusations! In fact, the experience was so strong that having no problems became a problem to me!

Now I know that when God speaks to me, His words are not just mere words but it is the Word, the Lord Himself, who carries life, love and wisdom beyond human understanding within Himself.

God began to teach me about it from that day. Today, I know that He never accuses or condemns me. God can admonish, instruct and rebuke but He will never accuse me. This is the devil's job.

He is the one who accuses me day and night[16]. Jesus, however, is constantly defending me[17]. He is my advocate, intercessor, spokesman and mediator. Is it not wonderful?

We can very easily observe how big an impact fear has on our relationship with God. Accusation is the main tool of the devil who is only waiting to intimidate us. Satan does everything possible so that we would feel accused and blame ourselves. This will cause us to be afraid to come to the Father. This is the first step to limit our relationship with God to make it a bond devoid of security and confidence.

The Holy Spirit is real person who can and wants to touch us just like any person. The Holy Spirit's touch is real, perceptible and tangible. But we close the way and confine our relationship with Him when we are afraid. It is as though we would say to Jesus: "Friendship is all that I can give you". Let's not talk to God that way. He does not want just our friendship, but He wants our whole heart and waits until we give ourselves completely to Him.

He waits for us to fall in love with Him and follow Him - let Him draw us.

Let us be bold in our relationship with God. Do not be afraid to give the Holy Spirit more room in your life and don't quench the Spirit when He wants to talk, touch and manifest Himself in all kinds of strange ways. Then our relationship with God will take on a new dimension and a new, deeper quality. Whenever any fear appears, we can freely say: "The Lord is the protector of my life! I will not be afraid!".

We will develop the subject of relationship with God and tell you about God as person in the next chapter. It is essential to have the image of a *personal God*, to know Him as someone who has feelings, a sense of humor, as someone who touches, talks, laughs and sings. Jesus is not a virtual power or philosophical truth. He is a Person. We will find out what this means in the next chapter.

---

[16]   Rev. 12:10

[17]   Heb. 7:25

Prayer

(*Lyrics*: Paul Oakley, Romance Me)

I need you like the summer needs the sun
I need you like a river needs the rain
I need you to fill me again
Without you, I run dry
Without you, I won't even survive

SO WAKE ME, TAKE ME WITH YOU
CHASE ME WHERE YOUR RIVER RUNS
ROMANCE ME 'TIL MY HEART BELONGS
TO YOU

THINK IT OVER ONE MORE TIME

➤ What does the Bible say about the Holy Spirit in John 7:37-39?

➤ Did anyone ever accuse or condemn you of anything? What was your reaction?

➤ What helps us not to be afraid of God?

➤ How many times did God say in Scriptures, *Do not be afraid*? What does it mean for us today?

➤ Are you ready to say today, "Holy Spirit came as you want? I come to you by the blood of Jesus. I ask you to touch me, change me and cause me to fall in love with you."

In the thirtieth year, on the fifth day of the fourth month, while I was among the exiles at the Kebar River, the heavens opened and I saw a divine vision. (On the fifth day of the month—it was the fifth year of King Jehoiachin's exile— the word of the LORD came to the priest Ezekiel the son of Buzi, at the Kebar River in the land of the Babylonians. The hand of the LORD came on him there). As I watched, I noticed a windstorm coming from the north—an enormous cloud, with lightning flashing, such that bright light rimmed it and came from it like glowing amber from the middle of a fire.

Above the platform over their heads was something like a sapphire shaped like a throne. High above on the throne was a form that appeared to be a man. I saw an amber glow like a fire enclosed all around from his waist up. From his waist down I saw something that looked like fire. There was a brilliant light around it, like the appearance of a rainbow in the clouds after the rain. This was the appearance of the surrounding brilliant light; it looked like the glory of the LORD. When I saw it, I threw myself face down, and I heard a voice speaking.

(Ezekiel 1:1-4, 26-28, NET Bible)

6

GOD WHO SEES, HEARS, SPEAKS AND TOUCHES

How cruel it is to believe in God who cannot touch.
How much more cruel is to believe in God whose touch
is nothing more than what this world has to offer.

If we were to ask Christians today, 'What is God like, or what God do you know?', I suppose the replies would mostly include fairly vague answers taken directly from church pulpits: "God is good", "God is great", "God is wonderful". Well yes, this is an obvious truth but the question is not: *What is God like?*, but rather: *What God do you know?*.

Christianity without a personal knowledge of God as a person becomes mere ideology and a belief in someone presented in fairytales. Until we meet with God as a real person, we won't be able to answer even in a few sentences about who and what *my* God is like.

It is as though someone would introduce me to another person saying that she is wonderful and suits me perfectly. I would agree to meet her, however, our relationship would be based solely on stories I have heard about her from someone else. If a few years later someone asks me what I think about my "friend', of course I could say a few things, but it wouldn't result from my *personal* relationship with her. It would only be based on what other people had told me.

Relationship with Jesus is the same – we can also talk about Him only based on what we have heard, not knowing what He is really like. This is so sad.

When an atheist says, 'there is no God', I don't judge this based on his and my arguments. I do not attempt to understand his rational reasoning. I shrug my shoulders and reply: "The problem is that if you would like to convince me that there is no God, you would first have to prove to me that you do not exist." What an absurd thought! How come? Why? Because to me, the existence of God is not a matter of arguments but knowledge of a particular *person*. For me it is not a matter of belief or being right. I know God the way I know every person. I can say what His voice is like and what I feel when He talks to me. I know what is He like when I'm upset, how happy He is and how He cries. I also know how great is His power and glory. It is impossible to convince someone that you do not exist. In the same way I cannot be convinced that God does not exist – *the person I know*.

We have a completely different approach to a relationship with someone after experiencing something with him or her. Until we look into each other's eyes and say what we think, until we ask for what we want and ask for something specific, we will never be able to say what we really know about a person. I would like to tell about three extremely meaningful stories at this point.

There is a German saying that says that one man presumed that his ax was stolen by his neighbor's son. From that time the man began to perceive him as a thief. Whatever the neighbor's son did, it reminded the man of the stolen ax and brought back the thought that associated him with a thief. After few days the man found the ax in his own barn and finally stopped looking at the boy like a thief.

The lesson from this story is that we have a very serious tendency to hastily make conclusions based only on suspicions. But the problem is we will never be able to judge someone's heart based only on assumptions, and not knowing him *personally*.

The second, more powerful story is about a certain skinhead. It starts when this teenager gets seriously interested in the Nazi movement. After a few months the man joined an anti-Semitic organization that uses force in the fight against the Jews and *exterminates the inferior race*, as he called it. He hated Jews. He participated in marches, demonstrations, street fights and attacks on Jews. After several years of this kind of life he met and married a woman. One day his wife confessed to him she is Jewish by origin.

The man was very shocked but he loved his wife and began to investigate his background as well. Imagine his surprise when he discovered that his grandfather was also a Jew. He became interested in the history of Israel, he began to study the history of his nation and started to visit Jewish synagogues. After a few months he became a practicing Jew.

This story shows us that views themselves are dead and meaningless ideology apart from life and true knowledge. The shocking thing about this story is the fact that the man for nearly ten years of his life hated people who it turned out he was one of! And he did it only because he was taught to do so.

The third story is taken from an old and very inspiring movie. It tells of the friendship between a blind girl, Selina and an Afro-American she randomly met. It is an extremely touching movie. When her mother meets them in the park together, she shouts out loud, "Forget about this disgusting man". Several minutes later when talking with her friend, Selina utters one of the most poignant lines that I had the privilege to hear at the movies: "They all say this because they don't know you".

All three of these stories have one remarkable thing in common: it is very easy to judge another person by appearances, characteristics or our knowledge about some people. It is easy to display negative conclusions, judge and discriminate. It all derives from a *lack of personal knowledge*. When we personally get to know someone, *knowledge about* that person disappears and ceases to be relevant. From that point what we think about that person comes from our *relationship* with the person.

The same is with the Lord God. We can talk about Him and carry on discussions with people about Him; however, until we get to know Him, our image of Him will only be based on *knowledge* rather than *relationship with God.*

I happened to talk with my colleagues from work who declared their atheism quite clearly, "God does not exist because priests are such and such, and the Church is a dead institution with the sole purpose of making money." There are thousands of similar arguments out there. I am even willing to affirm them sometimes but I disagree that God does not exist.

The church as an institution may cease to exist as far as I am concerned. All people can deny their faith and conclude that church organization is fiction. However, faith in doctrine or institutionalism is not the foundation for me. Faith in the living God is.

Jesus Christ is the foundation of my faith - The real person of Jesus. It is not a matter of allegations and unverified human stories. Jesus is alive because I know Him - as the One who sees, hears, feels, speaks and touches. I am not one of those who laugh at unbelievers and claim in empty arrogance that they are fools because they do not have a clue of what they talk about. Not at all. They do know what they talk about. The Church, on the other hand, must admit its weaknesses.

I worked with the youth in the church when I was in my twenties. It was a wonderful time in my life and I will never forget many wonderful meetings with passionate young people. I will never forget the trips we took together, late-night prayers and long conversations on Biblical matters.

There was a very important thing I noticed at that time: the major problem is not that young people (and not only) do not want to attend the church and prefer to spend time on entertainment or surfing the Internet. The main reason for this state is the lack of knowledge of God as a person and, therefore, lack of experience that would supersede all the entertainment and things we encounter in daily living.

I think it is cruel to believe in God, who cannot touch us. However, even crueler is to believe in God whose touch is nothing more than what the world can offer us. The church needs the touch of God. The church needs relationship with God that goes beyond all that the system of this world has to offer us.

The Holy Spirit wants us to know the Father by the fact that we will seek Him with *all our hearts* and we will taste how good He is rather than being someone who is only mentioned in stories. If only there was more said at Church about God, who and what He is, unbelievers would perceive the Church in a completely different way. Moreover, there would not be any doubt as to whether what the world has to offer is any better than what the Lord can give us. We would know His true love and we would be confident in His goodness that far exceeds all that we could experience from this world.

> *I have set the Lord always before me;*
> *Because He is at my right hand I shall not be moved.*
> *Therefore my heart is glad, and my glory rejoices;*
> *My flesh also will rest in hope.*
> *For You will not leave my soul in Sheol,*
> *Nor will You allow Your Holy One to see corruption.*
> *You will show me the path of life;*
> *In Your presence is fullness of joy;*
> *At Your right hand are pleasures forevermore.* (Ps. 16:8–11 NKJV)

God desires this joy and delight for each of us already here on earth. His desire is not just for us to wait for life after death, singing that life down on Earth is nothing but toil, drudgery and tears, and if I endure, perhaps I shall see the Lord. We cannot spend our lives waiting for something that is to come. God is available for us today. He greatly desires for us to know Him and experience His love, goodness, pleasure and glory. In Psalm 36 we read:

> *How precious is Your lovingkindness, O God!*
> *Therefore the children of men put their trust under the*
> *shadow of Your wings.*

They are abundantly satisfied with the fullness of Your house,
And You give them drink from the river of Your pleasures.
For with You is the fountain of life;
In Your light we see light.
Oh, continue Your lovingkindness to those who know You,
And Your righteousness to the upright in heart. (Ps. 36:7-10 NKJV)

There are numerous passages in the Bible that talk about kindness, pleasure and intimacy but we rarely talk about them. However, God does not want to limit our relationship with Him only to a monologue and fulfillment of the most important religious ceremonies. The Lord wants us to be saturated with the *river of His pleasures.* Have we ever pondered that? The great and sometimes unavailable God has these things called *pleasures.* He does not set any boundaries before us. His arms are open and waiting for us to fall into them, snuggle up to our Daddy, cry, laugh, listen, speak, be changed, consoled and tenderly touched.

This image of God is the most appropriate – the Father who hears, listens, speaks, touches, hugs, heals and gives hope. His rivers of pleasure go far beyond the comprehension of pleasure in terms of an imperfect human body. It is something that transcends the comprehension of the human mind.

In the sphere of the flesh man is very sensitive to what affects our senses, but God's touch is another kind of touch – one that starts from the inside out. The pleasures of the world are temporary and always leave behind a bitter aftertaste of painful consequences. The pleasures of God are eternal and leave behind a taste of heaven – a revelation of eternity.

Recently, I saw something in the Bible that I hadn't noticed before although I had read it dozens of times. I was very pleased by the message of this passage.

Do not love the world or the things in the world. If anyone loves the world, the love of the Father is not in him. For all that is in the world — the lust of the flesh, the lust of the eyes, and the pride of life — is not of the Father but is of the world. And the world is passing away, and the lust of it; but he who does the will of God abides forever. (1 John 2:15-17, NKJV).

These few lines contain the answer to half of the problems Christian face: "the world is passing away, and the lust of it".

We can feel unappreciated, thus we'll try doing anything in order to be regarded as great in the eyes of this world. But the Bible says it will pass. We can live in the lusts of the flesh overwhelmed by our fleshly desires but the Bible says it will pass as well. We can acquire education just to feel better[18]. We can build larger and more comfortable houses, buy faster cars, take out loans and still have growing needs despite the fact that we have everything necessary for life. However, all that will also pass. We can be famous, rich and feel physically attractive[19]. This too will pass.

God unveils His heart to us. He wants us to do His will – love Him and get to know Him without waiting for life after death. That is something that will never pass away. This word is very encouraging. Almost every problem involves three areas of our life: lust of the flesh, lust of the eyes and the pride of life. When we remember this verse and start to live it, we will be freed from all worries and concerns because our eyes will be focused on Jesus. The world and everything in it is passing away but we will abide forever.

Some Christians believe that God speaks to us only through the

---

[18]   Acquiring education is not wrong within itself. However, when we put our trust in it, motivated by a desire to be great and recognized, it certainly is not good. In everything we need to have pure motivations according to the will of God.

[19]   Here I am referring to the cult of the body, which is very prevalent in today's media. This cult goes far beyond the true and healthy concept of beauty found in the Bible.

prophets. When I was seventeen I wanted to go to a conference so much because I wished God would say something to me by one of the people ministering there. I dreamed about it and I was waiting for it. However, nobody said anything to me and I went back marveling that God did not speak to me. Jesus does not communicate with us like this. Of course, prophecies should be important to us but the most important thing is always what the Holy Spirit speaks to us.

He wants to talk but he needs our presence. God desires to touch us but it requires our time. God wants to be intimate with us but He needs love and devotion. He cannot do it without us.

Sometimes it seems to us that only great followers of Jesus can hear God. We think we are unworthy, too weak and have no chance to "break through" to God. We treat Him as the President – at the most you can only shake hands with him if you are lucky. But who were Lazarus, Martha, Mary, Zacchaeus, Magdalene, the disciples of Jesus and many others? They were ordinary people who often struggled with serious problems, lack of social approval and did not have a high social status. They were just like us. They were just like *you and me.*

When I first told myself I will look for God, I spent exactly an hour a day doing so. After one hour I would leave, close the door and return to my regular responsibilities. After a few months of regular prayer I noticed something changed inside me. I started to think about God more often. My thoughts would wander toward Him even though I would still end my prayer after an hour, close the door and return to my day-to-day responsibilities. One day I realized I was longing for prayer - I was missing God! Months had passed and my longing was increasing. Eventually, it came to the point that there was nothing I would not talk to God about. During the day I would think about what I wanted to talk about with my Dad in the evening and repeated it in my mind until we met. When I presented my problems to God, I would always receive an answer for everything.

Sometimes we think that prayer at a certain time does not make any sense because there is no Spirit in it. Nothing could be further from the truth. Of course, God does not care for our sense of duty but He cares for the heart. Often the initial obligation, however, turns into a fascinating relationship based on love, intimacy and trust.

Everything lies in sincere intentions and a true desire to know God.

If our love and passion are sincere, we can be sure that demonstrating perseverance will cause us to experience beautiful moments with our Lord.

The Holy Spirit was sent to comfort, help, support, add wisdom and protect us. We can always count on him. He is our Comforter, Helper, Counselor, Mediator and Advocate. The Holy Spirit was sent to reveal the love of the Father to us, to unveil the Scriptures before us and to always be there for us as our friend.

During times in my prayer closet I began to experience something completely new. Love appeared. It was a real, full and incredibly strong love. The Holy Spirit began to touch me, talk to me and hug me. I have never felt such love as the one I received from God. I have never experienced such great goodness and bliss before. I did not know this kind of love before. It was something that the world was not, is not and will not be able to offer me!

We will talk about God who is love in the next chapter. God is the personification of love, and His every part and feature is filled with love for man. This love is selfless, without conditions and demands. It is different than the love of man. This love is perfect because God Himself is its author and creator.

Prayer

(*Lyrics*: Vineyard, I Want To See You Now)

How can I know You more
Teach me who You really are
I want to come so close
Know how it feels to be loved
I WANT TO SEE YOU NOW
TOUCH YOUR FACE AND HOLD YOUR HAND
JESUS, JESUS
YOUR LOVE IS WONDERFUL TO ME

THINK IT OVER ONE MORE TIME

➢ What is your God like? Can you say something about God you know?

➢ Is there a difference between the knowledge of Jesus and the knowledge of Jesus in relationship? What is the difference?

➢ What is the foundation of your faith?

➢ What does God need to speak to us, touch us, cleanse and change us?

➢ Do you think the greatest pleasures offered to us by the world can compare to the *pleasures of God*? What are the differences between the pleasures of flesh and the *pleasures of God*?

For your sister Sodom was not a byword in your mouth in the days of your pride, before your wickedness was uncovered. It was like the time of the reproach of the daughters of Syria[a] and all those around her, and of the daughters of the Philistines, who despise you everywhere. You have paid for your lewdness and your abominations," says the Lord. For thus says the Lord God: "I will deal with you as you have done, who despised the oath by breaking the covenant. Nevertheless I will remember My covenant with you in the days of your youth, and I will establish an everlasting covenant with you. Then you will remember your ways and be ashamed, when you receive your older and your younger sisters; for I will give them to you for daughters, but not because of My covenant with you. And I will establish My covenant with you. Then you shall know that I am the Lord, that you may remember and be ashamed, and never open your mouth anymore because of your shame, when I provide you an atonement for all you have done," says the Lord God.'"

(Ezekiel 16:56–63, NKJV)

7

GOD WHO IS LOVE

One of the biggest lies of the devil is, "God does not love you anymore". Whenever I hear it, a completely different proclamation arises within me; "I have loved you with an everlasting love".

That's the very love of God. Whenever I read the sixteenth chapter of the Book of Ezekiel, I almost always have tears in my eyes. Is it possible for anyone to love that much? Is it possible for the love of God to be that big? Did God really forgive me of everything? What would a woman feel whose husband forgave all her abominations and betrayals? What would she think if she heard something similar to that in Ezekiel 16:62–63 (NASB): "May you be ashamed and never open your mouth because of your shame, because of the great love and forgiveness I have shown you."?

I'm not sure what she could really feel, but I do know such love is impossible from man's perspective. Only God can have such love. This is the kind of love that surpasses human understanding.

There are many love stories, poems and lines of poetry depicting perfect love, yet nobody has ever proven such love in the earthly realm. Human love always contains an element of imperfection. This is what makes us different from God. We are human and we are imperfect. No one will ever be able to love like Jesus did.

Selflessness is the first essential feature that distinguishes the love of the Father. God does not love us because we can offer Him something or because He needs something from us. God loves us because *we are*. This reason is good enough for Him.

God is the owner and the author of all things. There is nothing on the earth we could give Him that He doesn't have. Such a value does not exist. The Heavenly Father is completely self-sufficient. He does not need our love in order to live. He desires it. Man does not only desire love but needs it to live as well. That is what makes us different.

There are many documented cases of children who died from the lack of love when their mother abandoned them. They had food, they were warm and it seemed they had everything they needed. And yet they would die for completely unspecified reasons. Doctors diagnosed the cause of death as a result of the lack of love. Shocking, but true.

Also, it is not difficult to find people who did not have a sufficient amount of love in their childhood and to see how much devastation it caused in their lives. When we see human wrecks, often the cause of their downfall is the lack of love during childhood. Man needs love. That is how we were created.

Another feature that differentiates the love of God from human love is eternity. God has loved us with an everlasting love and there is no way for Him to stop loving us. There is nothing that can separate us from the love of God – even death.

> *Who is he who condemns? It is Christ who died, and furthermore is also risen, who is even at the right hand of God, who also makes intercession for us. Who Shall separate us from the love of Christ? Shall tribulation, or distress, or persecution, or famine, or nakedness, or peril, or sword? As it is written: "For Your sake we are killed all day long; We are accounted as sheep for the slaughter." Yet in all these things we are more than conquerors through Him who loved us. For I am persuaded That neither death nor life, nor angels nor Principalities nor powers, nor things present nor things*

*to come, nor height nor depth, nor any other created thing,
Shall be able that separate us from the love of God Which
is in Christ Jesus our Lord.* (Romans 8:34-39, NKJV)

Eternal love cannot be understood using the Greek way of
thinking. It should be accepted by the heart rather than trying to
comprehend it with the mind. When God loves us, He is never going
to give up on us even if we give up on Him. The Bible says *If we are
faithless, He remains faithful; He cannot deny Himself.* (2 Timothy 2:13,
NKJV). The Word of God says God cannot deny Himself. Why?
Because God is love. God cannot deny love because He is love. He
is the personification of love, each part of Him is love, His every
thought is love, every word and also every deed. Whatever God does,
He does it in and through love.

Perfect forgiveness is the next feature that distinguishes the
love of God. When God forgives us our sins, He erases them from
His memory and forgets them. Man is unable to forget. We must
admit we cannot forget when we think about rape, the Holocaust,
abuse during childhood, the alcoholism of a spouse, unpaid debt and
many other highly sensitive matters. In such cases, there is always
a cruel uncertainty regarding forgiveness. We may say we have
forgiven but we are forced to remember. Thinking about God we
can be absolutely confident that when He forgives, He forgets and
never recalls whatever He has forgiven. This is the perfect type of
forgiveness.

The first thing we expect after entering into a marriage
relationship is the mutual giving of each other and the sharing of
lives. Regret, remorse, accusation and often a divorce may take
place if a spouse does not give in enough. It is completely different
with God because His love is of different kind. The point is not that
God does not want our love and does not need it but there is not the
slightest remorse when He does not receive it from us. That is what
makes God's love different. Of course, in such cases He will be very
sad, crying and longing but He will never have regret, accusation,
condemnation or reproach against us. That is the way God is.

Man's relationship with God is also different from our relationship with another person. It is unequal and unfair – with the benefit for man. We may not spend our time with God, we may hurt and grieve Him, yet He will continue to love us with the same, complete and unwavering love. Problems begin when in marriage people start to live for themselves, expecting much of their spouse and demanding more than they give. With God it is different. The love of God is perfect and unchangeable regardless of whether God receives from us as much as we get from Him and regardless of whether we give Him as much as we expect of Him. It is extremely important to carry this truth in our hearts as security for the time when Satan will begin to sow doubts in us.

Many times I heard devil's standard accusation: "God doesn't love you anymore". What is even worse, I have heard similar sentences from the mouth of Christians directed towards others many times. This is very sad. If we cherish in our hearts the crucial revelation of God's love, such allegations will never have any effect on us. We need to be grounded in God, in other words, in His love. To be grounded is to have one hundred percent confidence and faith in the unchanging and unwavering love of God.

But can we believe it and accept it?

First of all there is a danger for man to have the attitude: God does not care for my sin and I have a full liberty to live in sin. However, this is complete nonsense. We do not have the liberty to sin but we can freely come to the Lord in spite of sin. The difference lies with having the proper perspective. The Bible says,

> *Or do you despise the riches of His goodness, Forbearance, and longsuffering, not knowing that the goodness of God leads you to repentance?* (Romans 2:4, NKJV)

When God shows love to us, we do not run away from Him but toward to Him. Today, a large number of people run away from God and, as a result, lose relationship with the Church. This is caused by the perspective of understanding God as One we should run away from while in sin. The Bible says, *Draw near to God and He will draw near to you* (James 4:8, NKJV). It also says, *and the one who comes to me I will by no means cast out* (John 6:37b, NKJV).

In spite of appearance, God sets no conditions but rather gives one hundred percent assurance: draw near and I will draw near to you, too. This sentence does not have any hidden content. This is what our God is like. And this is what He expects from us. He loves when we run to Him saying, "God, I failed you. I'm sorry but I am coming back to you." God will NEVER cast us away. His love is unconditional. Therefore, we cannot say, "God, please draw near to me". It does not work that way. He is always close, yet He always needs our closeness.

The second problem is the accusation about the lack of feeling God's love. Many atheists or agnostics claim there is no such thing as God's perfect love since it is impossible to feel it. Nothing could be further from the truth. God does not only let us feel His love but He also shows the superiority of His love over human love.

I will not forget the time in my life when I fell in love. Most of us have experienced this feeling. Falling in love is a time when almost every thought we think about is related to the other person. We become excited with just one thought about the person. We tremble and we are not fully rational because we idealize everything related to the object of our fascination in an unusual way.

But shortly after God came to me and showed me an even better kind of love: He caused me to fall in love with Him. It lasted for a few months during which God's love and His presence were physically felt even stronger than the presence of a beloved woman. My emotions seemed to be stronger than the emotions associated with anyone else. I was in love and nothing from the world had any value whatsoever. The lust of the flesh, the lust of the eyes and the pride of life did not exist for me.

Ever since, I've always said it is possible to be free from carnality. It can happen only when the awareness of God's presence is greater than the awareness of the presence of another human being. At that time the spiritual world is more real to us than the physical world and the unseen is more real than what is visible.

Faith in the love of God is one of the fundamental values of the Christian life. This is because, first of all, when the image of God's love is distorted the desire to know Him as Person is less, more distant and less desirable for us. There is no hunger for God in our hearts. Instead, there are other things more curious and fascinating to us. This is all due to the wrong perception of God's love.

The relationship between a father and a son conveys it best. When a father is, for us, the epitome of power and discipline, our desire to spend time with him is limited to short and perfunctory questions. We ask him about what is appropriate and what is not, what we should do and what to avoid. We also ask whether we did something well or not. Relationship with him is devoid of love and trust that is needed so much. The Lord desires much more for us. He desires love full of trust, devoid of fear and based on intimacy.

We often define God unilaterally; either as the God of mercy or as the God of judgment. But these two cannot be separated because God is not the God of mercy or the God of judgment only. He is the God of love. He is still the God of love, whether in mercy or in judgment.

God shows us mercy when we fail and make mistakes. He judges us only when we are too insensitive to accept His mercy. However, in both cases, the actions of God spring from love.

Sometimes people perceive the judgment of God in terms of cruelty or necessity – an act to "correct" us regardless of whether it will hurt us or not. However, this is not true. The judgment of God comes to turn us to the right paths full of goodness. God's judgment is always motivated by love. It is separation of sanctity from what is *unholy*. That is why our heart is the key. If we do not desire the true holiness of God, we will always have a problem with understanding His judgment.

The story of the woman caught in adultery is a confirmation of how much mercy dominates over judgment. This narrative tells us that the limits of our evil do not exist to God, nor do they change

His desire to protect us against rejection, hurt and damnation. God perfectly knows well what condemnation means in our life. It starts from an evil lie saying there is no hope for us and it all ends with our death. God does not want this for anybody but we must be grounded in God's love in order to know God's attitude when the devil comes whispering his lies in our ears.

First, we must not forget the precious blood of Jesus Christ. Its power and value are priceless and limitless. There is nothing in this world that is too bad to be forgiven.

Second, we must remember Him as a God of endless second chances. His love is eternal. When a friend lies to us a second, third and fourth time, we will eventually run out of patience and stop treating the words of such a person seriously. But God will never give up on us. He will wait for us *forever*.

I happened to read several times that God said to someone, "There is not any chance for this person any longer. Do not pray for them." Such words may only come from the accuser. God will never say anything like that to His child. He is the God of eternal love, endless second chances and He will never give up on you!

There is one more thing that makes the love of God different from human love. His love is devoid of the element of lust. The image of love has been devalued and the image of true love between two people has been even ravaged by distorting their beautiful feelings in an era of the media, the Internet and new technologies.

The Internet is full of licentiousness and perverse pornographic content. There is no love to it whatsoever, although, it is the result of a search for something more, something real as well as proof that every person has a need of experiencing true feelings. Mankind is created to love and destined to be loved. Everyone needs love just like they need water, sun and air. When love is missing, we fill the space with substitutes. However, nothing can match the love of Christ because this love is perfect. It is the love of the heart and not of the body.

And not only so, but in glory in tribulations also: knowing that tribulation worketh patience; And patience, experience; and experience, hope: And hope maketh not ashamed; because the love of God is shed abroad in our hearts by the Holy Ghost Which is given unto us. (Romans 5: 3‐5 KJV)

The media is full of stories of priests accused of pedophilia, experimenting in sexual contact with men and admitting using the services of prostitutes. This is horrible and tragic. It puts the true Church in a bad light and is often treated as an argument against the existence of God. However, none of it has anything to do with God. All such situations directly result from the lack of love that cannot be replaced with any substitute or temporary physical pleasure.

Whereas, the mystery of God's love lies in the fact that His love starts in our spirit, permeates the soul, mind, emotions and ends in the flesh. This kind of love satisfies all our desires, ensures peace, soothes pain as well as fills the emptiness and the need of being loved. Man's kind of love can only do that in a very limited manner. But God loves us in a complete and absolute way.

The Bible says:

Now before the feast of the Passover, when Jesus knew that his hour was come that he should depart out of this world unto the Father, having loved his own which were in the world, he loved them unto the end. (John 13:1, KJV)

No one is able to love us until the end except for Jesus.

There is another short story in the Bible that reveals the nature and size of Jesus' love for man.

Then Jesus beholding him loved him, and said unto him, One thing thou lackest: go thy way, sell whatsoever thou hast, and give to the poor, and thou shalt have treasure in heaven: and come, take up the cross, and follow me. And he was sad at that saying, and went away grieved: for he had great possessions. And Jesus looked round about, and saith unto his disciples, How hardly shall that they have riches enter into the kingdom of God! And the disciples were astonished at his words. But Jesus answereth again, and saith unto them, Children, how hard is it for them that trust in riches to enter into the kingdom of God! (Mark 10: 21-24, KJV)

This is a beautiful passage in the Word of God. How often do we have a problem with stopping our excitement, anger or frustration when we need to tell someone something that could touch him or her? Jesus shows us the pattern of how to He communicates with us regarding the things He does not like in us. Whenever He speaks to us He *loves us* first and as He speaks, He does it in love regardless of how serious and delicate the issue may be. Although the man from the parable had his hope in riches, He did not receive a harsh reprimand from the Lord nor did he hear any accusations. He *was loved* first instead.

This is what Jesus desires for us. Regardless of the place we are in or what have we done, before he does or says anything to us, first He *loves us.* And when He starts speaking, He will do it in love. This is the Jesus model of relationship with man.

Knowing God in His marvelous and great love is something substantial and significant. God's love has an impact on every aspect of life – it is a great force drawing us toward God rather than away from Him.

This is what love does when a moment of weakness or sin happens in the life of a Christian. We know which way we should run. We know that God's love is the best place where we can find refuge, receive forgiveness and fall into the arms of the loving Father just as the younger son did.

God not only wants to give us an accurate image of love but He desires for us to taste and experience that love. The taste of love will leave an indelible *mark* of the nature of God in us. We will never again have doubts as to its *greatness and fullness.*

In the next chapter we will talk about prayer. There is a lot being said today about a living relationship with Jesus. While talking with Christians from other denominations, we often come to the conclusion that it actually does not matter what church or denomination we represent. The most important thing is to have *a living relationship with God*. Therefore, we need to think about what a living relationship with God is and what is the model of prayer Jesus left for us.

Prayer

(Lyrics: Live Worship from the UK, How Good It Is)

O God of love, I come to you again knowing I'll find mercy.
I cannot explain all the things I see but
I'll trust in you in every moment you are there watching over,
HOW GOOD IT IS TO BE LOVED BY YOU
The hand of love giving power to overcome
if all beneath me falls away I know that you are God
Who can stand against me in my weakness,
you are strong, your love's everlasting

THINK IT OVER ONE MORE TIME

➤ *Name a few characteristics* that distinguish the love of God from human love.

➤ *What* is God's motivation in all He does for a man? Why is that?

➤ *Have you ever* been in love? Do you think falling in love with Jesus possible?

➤ *Do you believe in* the unconditional, eternal and complete love of God? What significance does it have for you?

And we have a dry trust through Christ toward God. Not that we are Sufficient of ourselves to think of anything as being from ourselves, but our sufficiency is from God, who also made us Sufficient as ministers of the new covenant, not of the letter but of the Spirit; [and] for the letter kills, but the Spirit gives life. But if the ministry of death, written and engraved on stones, was glorious, so that the children of Israel could not look steadily at the face of Moses because of the glory of his countenance, which glory was passing away, how will the ministry of the Spirit not be more glorious? For if the ministry of condemnation had glory, the ministry of righteousness exceeds much more in glory. For even what was made glorious had no glory in this respect, because of the glory that excels.

(2 Cor. 3:4-10, NKJV)

8

TRUE PRAYER

Prayer is the best way of achieving perspective that would be detached from worldliness and immersed in eternity.

Prayer is an extremely close matter to my heart. And it is not a matter of beautiful theories but rather a question of the role it plays in my life. To me, prayer is the link between the natural and the supernatural. It goes beyond the physical. It is the gateway leading to the courtroom of heaven - the nearest place to encounter God.

I believe that every time I open my mouth to pray the angels in heaven nudge each other and say, "Look, he is praying; see, he is crying; listen to him singing." The moment I start to pray the Holy Spirit's heart is filled with joy and willingness to be with me and to talk to me.

Prayer is a beautiful treasure given to us by the Father. We do not need to worry about whether we can pray or not because the Holy Spirit was sent to be our helper on earth. God has given us the opportunity to communicate in His wonderful language that is beyond human understanding. We have received it in order to proclaim the will of God in our lives.

Prayer is one of the most important indicatives of Christianity and the subject of countless lectures and sermons. Every Christian denomination has references to prayer. Regardless of how much is said about it or how it is perceived by Christian denominations, it has a different meaning and different dimension to each one. There are almost as many definitions of prayer as people. The secret, however, does not lie in a definition or in its meaning but in the heart, because prayer is not something of the mind but of the heart.

If I was asked, how many times did I hear in church that we all should pray more, I would honestly answer I do not remember, because it is being said all the time. This is the issue Christians are unanimous about. Almost every church continually repeats the words: "You should pray more."

Indeed, the fact is that prayer is essential in our lives and we won't build a relationship with Jesus without it. However, there is no mention about of a sense of responsibility or obligation. Thus, I am not saying that *I should pray* but I will rather hold to the fact that *I desire to pray, because* in prayer lies the greatest potential to know the true heart of the Father.

Today, a simple fact resulting from the obvious weakness of the flesh is that Christians have serious problems with managing time for prayer. The phrase, "It is not the quantity but the quality that matters" has firmly entered into the canon of the Protestant church. But truly God can be surprisingly flexible. Sometimes quantity leads to quality. But other times the quality is not enough due to the need for more quantity. There is no rule here. I remember how shocked I was when a man, who was one of my greatest spiritual authorities, confessed to praying only fifteen minutes a day. It only proves that each of us is in a different place with God and each of us has different needs in our relationship with Him.

God's standard of prayer is somewhat different. God desires something more. He desires us, our presence, our closeness and our hearts – not obligation. The Bible says,

Pray without ceasing (1 Thes. 5:17, KJV).

This is what is important to God. He is not impressed with the time and quantity of the words but with the heart, which is the spiritual perspective.

I mentioned earlier that when I first began to pray regularly I did it every day at specific times. I devoted an hour to God each day. Over time, my decision changed and I decided to I pray for an hour and a half. Sometime later I got an even better idea: I will pray for two hours and twenty-four minutes! That is the exact number of ten percent of the day. I said to myself: I will give God a tithe of my life! Oh, it will be so honorable and wonderful: I will give God as much as ten percent of my life! That is so amazing!

But I did not stop there. After several months my decision changed again. Tithing was not enough anymore and I did not want to be like the Pharisees. I wanted to be better than the Pharisees! So I decided that I would pray for four hours a day. Then, this was not enough for me either. So at one point I was praying so much that I did not have time for anything else. I was proudly setting the "records of prayer" with a watch in my hand.

Additionally, my prayer could not be silent. This became even a greater problem. If my prayer was to be non-verbal, how could it be called prayer! I had to speak some words to God for a few hours every day since I did not want to lie to others or myself.

One day I read in the Bible: *Pray without ceasing.* Oh no! That was too much. I was unable to meet this requirement. Why does God require so much of me? The answer was simple: He really does not require anything from me. This thought was like thunder from the sky. This revelation became obvious in just a moment. I could not stop laughing at myself. Surely, if I were to continue further in this line of thought, I'd have to become a hermit in order to find enough time to pray. Obviously, I would not be able to finish my school, go to work or start a family.

Also, I remember a certain "honorable brother" who was more desperate than me and there was nothing that could discourage him. It happened a few years before I read this simple verse in the Letter to the Thessalonians. I was young at that time and I just thought:

"This pastor is really determined!" Our conversation started with him saying three times, "glory to God" and five times "Hallelujah" before he asked any questions. And when answering a question, he would say something like, "Thank you, Jesus. I praise you, Jesus" before and after the answer.

It would not be a problem if he would keep his prayers to God, rather than proclaiming them to the whole world.

As you can see, there are different degrees and dimensions of spiritual advancement. Of course, far be it from me to speak even one word of criticism against that man. However, this is not at all the kind of prayer Jesus requires from us.

Today when I think about it, I see how God is devoid of formalism. That is the God I know. He is not a God who demands perfectness of us, but He is a Father who is interested in our hearts more than discipline.

I often meet people whose hard work leads to great professional success. They become famous, loved and popular. They owe almost everything to their hard work.

In prayer, it is difficult to separate the effort from the effects of your "work". However, there is a fundamental difference between perfectionism, workaholism, and the purity of heart. The Bible does not say, *blessed are the workaholics and perfectionists*, but it says, *blessed are the pure in heart, for they shall see God*. You can be a perfectionist, workaholic and a man of great discipline, but not have a *pure heart*. That is when the problem starts.

Perfection may be the biggest obstacle in knowing the Holy Spirit. We tend to forget that sometimes it is good to give up our own plans for a *pure heart*.

The undeniable truth is that God gives us priceless gifts from *His goodness*. Our heart is the only criterion here. It says, *I am nothing and I am nobody, so come and use my nothingness*. This is the attitude of a true servant regardless of where he is in life; whether he is fifteen years old and starts his search for God or he is a merited servant of God. If such an attitude is foreign to us, this means we have crossed the frontier of our greatness at some point. Greatness cannot be created based on our own excellence. Greatness is founded in our identity in Jesus. The Bible says,

> *Wherefore let him thinketh he standeth That take heed lest he fall (1 Cor. 10:12, KJV). Let no man deceive himself. If any man among you seemeth to be wise in this world, let him become a fool, that he may be wise (1 Cor. 3:18, KJV). But so shall it not be among you: but whosoever will be great among you, shall be your minister: And whoever of you will be the chiefest, shall be servant of all. (Mark 10:43-44, KJV).*

When we start to assign anything to ourselves it has nothing to do with the greatness we have in Christ. Greatness only comes through serving in everything we do, even if it seems to be irrational for us. Greatness is serving without a desire for glory. It is identification with Jesus as the source of everything because He is the One who bestows glory.

There is a very fine line between receiving glory from people and giving glory to God. Sometimes, we give glory to God but accept the greater glory from men. This is not right. The Lord wants all the glory because He does not share His glory with anyone.

We must have unwavering confidence that it is only because of God that we stand, we are and we exist. A great man does not think he stands due to his own strength. Rather, he acknowledges God to be his sustainer – He is his rock and source of everything. Finally, the goal for serving should not be people's applause but God's approval, since the Lord is the only One who justly measures and rewards.

Sometimes we are convinced we have achieved everything because we get such feedback from people. We may also think we are *great* because the multitudes convince us we are. However, the best measure of our worth is really the voice of the Holy Spirit and not man. Following the voice of a man rather than the Spirit may turn out to be very deceptive.

We can only be great when we are simple servants whose ministry is to respond to the Word. Every greatness in this world is small in the eyes of God.[20] Whatever is meaningless in this world is great in the sight of God. Our weakness and "smallness" is the place from which we can draw the greatest blessing.

We do not need to run away from greatness. We are to be small even where the greatest human greatness manifests itself.

The true value of our achievements will be revealed in eternity. All that we see and experience on earth is indeed a shadow of the things to come.

The best thing we can do is to guard the innermost motives of our actions and care for the purity of heart by constantly asking God which motivations in us are incorrect. We must ask what indicators and intentions focus on the effects of what we do and our own glory rather than service[21]. God will not allow taking the glory that is due Him. This is an extremely sensitive matter to our Lord.

Martin Luther said, *Pray as if all of your work did not matter and work as if prayer was useless.* This is the best definition of separation between spirituality and the physical life. God does not expect us to be spirits because we live in the flesh but He also desires our prayers more than anything else. Jesus knows that prayer is the only place of direct contact with Him. Hence, the conclusion that sometimes Christians tend to "spiritualize" things that have nothing to do with spirituality.

For example, when someone is trying to rob us, we don't say that this is appropriate because that is how God is teaching us humility.

---

[20] This doesn't have to do with sickness or the things in which God has nothing in common.

[21] Of course, we also live in the flesh and I do not mean to abuse on formal matters. We need to separate spirituality issues from pure pragmatism. For example, if someone tries to cheat us regarding financial matters, serving here will not be the best solution to the problem. In everything we need balance and the common sense of the Holy Spirit.

Another thing is that God has nothing to do with religion. The indicators and intentions of our hearts are always the most important for Him. Thus, even though sometimes we do things against all logic and human approval, being at loss in the material realm, we can be sure that when we do it in the simplicity of the heart and trusting God, He will bless in due time. Our Lord is very flexible.

On the other hand, let us forget about the problems and matters that fill our minds so much when we pray.

That was one of the biggest problems during my prayers for the first time. The mouth would speak the words but the mind was preoccupied with hundreds of other issues. The solution to this problem lies within a simple thing: *not giving up.* We don't give ourselves a chance to change when we conclude it is pointless. However, when we will constantly talk to the Holy Spirit that we want something more – that is when things start to happen! The Lord will begin to give us things that go beyond our imagination or dreams. Jesus said:

> *And when thou prayest, thou shalt not be as the hypocrites are: for they love to pray standing in the synagogues and in the corners of the streets, that they may be seen of men. Verily I say unto you, they have their reward. But thou, when thou prayest, enter into thy closet, and when thou hast shut thy door, pray that thy Father which is in secret; and thy Father seeth in secret which shall reward thee openly. But when ye pray, use not vain repetitions, as the heathen to: for they think they that shall be heard for their much speaking. Be not ye therefore like unto them: for your Father knoweth what things ye have need of, before ye ask him* (Matthew 6: 5-8, KJV).

There are three main topics within this passage: "hiding", "reticence" and "fatherhood". The prayer model Jesus left with us consists of these three components. Intimacy does not appear until we enter the hiding place with the Father - the place of reticence. Jesus does not desire our words as much as our hearts. This is the biggest secret of relationship with Him.

The Polish Bible translation of the eighth verse subtly misleads us. While it says nothing about God the Father but only the *Father* in a number of verses earlier, the term *God the Father* appears in the eighth verse. The original translation does not have the word "God" here, which is very important at this point. Our Lord does not want us to treat Him as a *distanced God* in relationship with Him. He wants us to see Him as a *close Father*, whose attitude toward us is not based on power but on *fatherly love.*

The hiding place is essential in our relationship with the Father. We can pray for hours at conferences, in church or at prayer meetings. But our relationship with the Father will be limited until we enter the hiding place. It is in the hiding place where intimacy is produced. The exact same principle applies to marriage. I cannot imagine intimacy between spouses who never had time to be together by themselves – in a hiding place. So it is with our heavenly Father.

Very often we treat the Father as our last source of salvation. There is nothing wrong with us running to Him at a time of need but that is not what the Father longs for. Many of us are called to do great things and we are endowed with tremendous anointing, however, we only pray when we need it. It is sad, but nonetheless the Father always waits for us with open arms. He waits for our presence because He desires it more than we desire His.

Jesus desires our presence so that He could come to us. Therefore, if we want the presence of God, we have to find time to *commune* with God. Relationship with Jesus is not one-way. There are two essential elements required: *God's presence* and *my presence.*

A relationship with God which does not include an element of His intervention in our lives is called a one-way relationship or one-sided. A one-sided relationship cannot be based on love because love is never one-sided. A true relationship with God grants Him permission to carry out reforms in our lives. It is not only about talking to Him, but also listening and doing whatever He asks us to do.

When the Bible speaks of hiding, there is no mention of it being a command. It would be as though we were saying to an engaged couple that if they want to see each other, then they can only do so at a designated place. There needs to be balance.

Intimacy with God is a process rather than following commands. It is just like in a relationship with a future spouse – we need much time to be together alone in the beginning. We need to get to know each other. At this stage, we learn to trust God and know His heart. When we pass this stage, we will be able to enjoy intimacy in places of which we would have never even thought.

I remember several occasions when the closeness of God was extremely strong. However, it was not at church or at home. Some examples have been in an elevator, in the forest, in a field, in a car or even in the bathroom. This is the place the Holy Spirit wishes to bring us to – a relationship at the level of the spirit. The hiding place with Jesus is something much bigger and deeper than just spending time with Him behind the closed doors of a room. Unceasing prayer is the state of our spirit. That is the answer to the question: How is it possible to pray without ceasing? It is only through the spirit.

A few years ago, during a fierce debate on a controversial subject at a home group meeting, I felt some words deep inside me. I did not hear them physically but I felt my spirit talking to God despite the fact that I was saying something to the group at that time. That is when I felt that Holy Spirit speaking to me: *This is that kind of prayer.*

It was unbelievable! Even though I was talking to people, I felt like my spirit was intensely praying at the same time. This is the kind of prayer Jesus preached about and what He taught His disciples. When Jesus said, "*In this manner, therefore, pray*" and then He uttered the most famous prayer in the history of mankind, He did not mean to repeat a formula in order to meet a religious obligation. There was something more profound to it. Jesus meant a heart attitude that repeats these words in every moment of life, "Our Father in heaven, hallowed be Your name. Your kingdom come and be revealed here."

If today's church functioned more on the principle of *spiritual serving* rather than religious formulas, it would be surprised with the results that such ministry provides. Wherever we would go we would see the effects of Jesus' prayer. The name of God would be honored and revered, the Kingdom of God would be revealed in great power, the will of God would be fulfilled and we would live in forgiveness. That was the intention of Jesus.

When Jesus was on the earth before He began his ministry, He spent more time in prayer and less time with the people. Was it a coincidence? Certainly not. Jesus desired *constant prayer*. In Luke we read:

> *Watch ye therefore, and pray always, that ye may be accounted worthy to escape all these things that shall come to pass, and to stand before the Son of man. And in the day time he was teaching in the temple; and at night he went out, and abode in the mount that is called the mount of Olives. And all the people came early in the morning to him in the temple, for to hear him.* (Luke 21:36-38, KJV).

It is interesting that Jesus said to *pray always*, and yet He prayed mostly at night. However, that is the model our Lord left with us. We are to pray without ceasing and moreover designate a special time to *meet* with the Father. True prayer does not work only in one of those areas. We need prayer of the heart and a time alone with God. We need prayer in the spirit and a face-to-face meeting. Otherwise, we may be exposed to danger. It is impossible to know the Father without meeting Him, because it is like comparing a relationship between a father and a son who do not see each other at all. What would such a relationship look like? It would not result from *knowing the Father* but rather from *knowledge about the Father*.

Humility is one of the things we need most in our relationship with the Holy Spirit. Prayer is the best means and tool leading to humility. It is during prayer that we learn humbleness and humility. We need to come to the place of humility and first strip away our pride in order to meet Jesus and get to know Him. The Bible says that God avoids the proud but gives grace to the humble. Prayer is what paves the way for us to taste humility. This is where the longest journey through the world of God's greatness begins.

I have a few extremely strong testimonies on this subject from my own life. One of them concerns a huge embarrassment I experienced when I got a job that was a great personal failure to me – offending my pride. I have always treated myself as a person with higher ambitions, who would never lower myself to the level of physical work. Shortly after, I got a job with which I was disgusted. Also, my salary was so ridiculously low it was difficult to even imagine. I felt debased when acquaintances would pass me by and smile seeing me at work. I experienced humiliation.

God would speak to my heart in spite of such a difficult time, saying there are people who find themselves in even worse situations. I knew I had to act according to this word.

We must somehow react when things like these happen in our lives. That is why I would buy candy bars and give them to people whose life situations seemed to be even more hopeless. I think I will never forget about a family that accepted candy bars from me and said; *Thank you so much. We have never eaten such things.* I knew heaven would open over me then. God does not give us trials and tests to humiliate us but to shape us and draw us closer to Him as well as to reassure our hearts and give us more of Himself.

Just after three months I got a job where I earned several times more and worked several times less. God taught me a principle at that time: *When you taste humiliation and embarrassment, when you are facing a period of great difficulties - be sure that something you have never dreamt about will happen soon.* That is why whenever difficulties appear in my life I always know God is preparing something extraordinary and special[22]. It is a good time! Great things are coming!

These are the things that happen when we pray. They are a direct result of our prayers. God cares for us and makes sure that we would always be able to know Him better. But none of this will happen without humility because this is the path to the blessings and greatness of God. Human reputation is merely what people think about us. However, true greatness lies in the way God sees our hearts. Human reputation is not always right because it is not based on the motivations of the heart but rather on outward circumstances. God's reputation is excellent.

---

[22]   Of course, provided that we use this time to get closer to God and our actions are an expression of faith in God's protection and the belief that everything belongs to God and is His property.

The form of prayer is also an important matter. We often hear about what prayer should look like, how loud we should pray and how we should behave during prayer. I was deeply involved in this model, I must admit. I probably broke and exhausted all the possible conventions and good manners in my life with God – meaning good manners from man's perspective because such a set of standards does not exist to God. It is people who are trying to put Him in a box and nicely wrap it. However, the Holy Spirit is not the God of a set pattern but freedom.

Several times I was shouting so loudly to God that my body refused to work. Not only my throat but my whole body! I was shouting so loudly that I fell down exhausted and weak. The Bible says:

> *I am weary with my crying; my throat is parched.*
> *My eyes grow dim with waiting for my God*
> (Psalm 69:3-4, RSV).

And,

> *I cry aloud to God, aloud to God, that he may hear me.*
> (Ps 77:2, RSV).

As you can see, there is nothing wrong with crying aloud to God. There is though a difference between crying aloud to God and shouting at God. Crying and shouting are expressions of our desperation and determination. *I will not be silent* – these are the words often spoken by the psalmists. They did not want to be found in a place where God would not hear their hearts because they knew at that time they needed God more than ever before.

God is not deaf and He can hear our every whisper and every thought. However, we must remember that He also looks at our determination and it is often measured by shouting.

There are moments when all that we need in our lives is silence. Bible verses can be found regarding this:

Rest in the Lord, and wait patiently for Him (Psalm 37:7, NKJV).
Be angry, and do not sin.
Meditate within your heart on your bed, and be still.
Offer the sacrifices of righteousness and put your trust in the Lord (Psalm 4:4-5, NKJV).

Different churches and denominations have developed their own canon of prayer. Some will try to convince us that shouting is from the devil and that it is wrong. On the other hand, others claim you cannot be silent in prayer. I got familiar with the teaching that says prayer should be based on a so-called *quiet time*. There is nothing wrong with this until we make it the rule. We can have a quiet time with God but sometimes it happens that we need something more. There are moments in life when according to what the psalmists wrote *we cannot be silent* due to some things which make you shout to the Lord and rend your heart before Him.

The most precise and a yet simple form of prayer is expressed in the Book of Ecclesiastes:

A time to keep silence, and a time to speak (Ecclesiastes 3:7, NKJV).

There is a time to keep silent and a time to speak in the life of each of us. The same is true in our relationship with God. Sometimes we may be silent but it also happens that our shouts are moving heaven. We don't have to be afraid that there is something wrong with this. Jesus loves watching us as we pour our hearts out before Him.

In chapter two, we said a few words about openness. The attitude of an open heart is the most important thing in our relationship with God because we cannot receive what He desires to give us unless our hearts are open. Actually, openness leads to submission, which is the key to true intimacy. It is the reflection the Lord Himself looks through at our hearts. Submission attracts the Holy Spirit.

Without humility there is no openness. Without openness there is no submission. Without submission there is no intimacy.

Even though it is widely discussed, prayer for many Christians is only a religious duty that does not add anything to our lives. We treat prayer as a necessary good rather than something to be desired. Many teenagers spend their youth on getting as much pleasure out of life as possible. But when prayer is mentioned, they smile in irony and say, "What will prayer give me? What is the benefit of talking to someone I cannot see?". We would like to get something from God and then live our own lives. But God does not work that way. God not only wants to give us something but He desires for us to know Him. This is the greatest mystery of prayer. There is no point to receiving anything from God if we don't know Him. It is like a European citizen who has a son in Australia and tries to build a relationship with his son by sending gifts through the post office. But can someone build a distant relationship with the Father by only accepting His gifts?

We need to know the Father in order for His gifts to begin to make sense to us. When we receive a gift but don't know the person who gave it to us, the value of the gift is insignificant to us. It is not the expression of love but only a physical object. The same is with God. He desires to work with us based on intimacy rather than the give and take principle. We can be sure we are in the right place of prayer only when the giving and receiving results from intimacy.

That is why it is so important to learn the rule: I am not to look at what I receive or if there are any wonderful experiences with God but rather to believe that He exists and rewards those who seek Him. If we apply this principle, we can be one hundred percent sure that the day will come when the Holy Spirit will surprise us. He will bring us to the place of extraordinary glory. We will start crying to God saying we do not want to have anything to do with this world and that we want to be there with Him now. This is the place Paul talked about: *that the children of Israel could not look steadily at the face of Moses because of the glory of his countenance, which glory was passing away, how will the ministry of the Spirit not be more glorious? For if the ministry of condemnation had glory, the ministry of righteousness exceeds much more in glory. For even what was made glorious had no glory in this respect, because of the glory that excels. For if what is passing away was glorious, what remains is much more glorious.* (2 Cor. 3:7b-11, NKJV).

This is the glory our Father desires for each of us. He wants to lead us into the court of heaven where His glory is imperishable and surpasses by far the glory from the Old Testament. This is the result of the New Covenant and ministry in the realm of the spirit. This is what we should strive and seek for in order to enter the dwelling place of the Holy Spirit.

There is a prayer that results from knowing the Person of Jesus and a prayer that results from a sense of an obligation. However, the Lord is waiting for the time when we will not speak the words we do not understand out of obligation. He wants each word spoken in prayer to be meaningful and to result from the revelation of His person to us.

For certain prayer is an extraordinary and beautiful treasure given to us on earth by the Father. It is the most wonderful spiritual tool in the hand of a Christian. Whatever arises in prayer is legitimate and great. Anything born during prayer has tremendous power for breakthroughs in our lives. All thoughts, conclusions, decisions and changes that happen in prayer are mighty and have unlimited power to change the reality around us. The greatest spiritual potential and true authority of God in us is conferred during prayer. And finally, prayer is a time to communicate with God Himself. It is a time when revelation comes down straight from heaven to fill our lives and overflow to everything we touch.

Prayer is supernatural and great. The greatest spiritual breakthroughs happened as a result of prayer. The greatest revivals and the most important turning points in history took place through prayer. Prayer is the factor with the greatest potential. It allows for transition from the visible to the invisible and from the temporal to the eternal. It is the best way to acquire perspective detached from earthliness and immersed in the atmosphere of heaven.

In the next chapter we will continue our discussion on prayer and turn our focus to worship. Prayer and worship of the Father are the two indivisible issues. We cannot worship God without prayer nor can we separate prayer from worship. Otherwise, it would be limited to asking and would not be a dialogue but only a monologue. In turn, no monologue makes a relationship but rather division. When prayer and worship is limited to a monologue, they limit our Christianity as well. It becomes empty, idle and devoid of life. Whereas Christ is our life and our relationship with Him is the greatest thing we have in life.

The church has become accustomed to combining worship with music. Therefore, we'll think about the role of music in worship. Is worship more than just words? How can we go deeper in worshipping God? What type of worship model did Jesus give us?

Prayer

(Lyrics: Planetshakers, Don't Pass Me By)

I'm reaching out
I'm waiting here for more
For more of You

Cause all I want is You
And all I need is to be here with You

I'M HUNGRY FOR YOUR FIRE
I'M DESPERATE, YOU'RE MY ONE DESIRE
JESUS, PLEASE DON'T PASS ME BY

THINK IT OVER ONE MORE TIME

➢ *In* the context of prayer, what do you think about this statement: "It is not the quantity but the quality that matters"?

➢ What is *God's standard* of prayer according to 1 Thess. 5:17?

➢ Is shouting to God wrong? How can you explain it? Have you ever shouted to God?

➢ *Why is prayer* so important in the Christian life?

➢ *What* does God desire the most in prayer?

But the hour is coming, and now is, when the true worshipers will worship the Father in spirit and truth; for the Father is seeking such to worship Him. God is Spirit, and those who worship Him must worship in spirit and truth.

(John 4:23-24, NKJV)

9

THE HIGHEST WORSHIP PLACE

The highest worship place is where God can smell a pleasant fragrance. However, there is no fragrance without a sacrifice and there is no sacrifice without a fire and a real death.

I am terrified by one thought when I wonder sometimes about how the church would look without worship. The change would not be too significant. It is because most of us associate worship only with music. What would happen if the music was taken away? What would the Church be like if there was no electricity or all of the instruments were stolen?

The form or content is not the most valuable thing in worship of the Father. It is the pleasant fragrance that comes from our hearts. The Lord does not expect perfection and excellence from His worshipers nor does He expect any special artistic setting or erudition. He desires to inhale a pleasing fragrance. However, it cannot be found in music or the sounds of instruments. God smells the fragrance of our hearts. To worship Him is to stand before Him in spirit and in truth.

A number of musicians may be slightly offended by this point but the fact is that music is only the *means* and the *tool* to release our hearts in worship. It is not the *goal* in itself.

It may seem odd but singing does not mean worshiping. When I hear people talk about the "worship team" in churches, I think sometimes we have the wrong concept. The Bible never uses such terminology.

There is a considerable difference between a team of singers, musicians, and the worship team. The misunderstanding that has crept in at this point has distanced us from true worship - the model that Jesus left with us. The term "worship team" does not exist in God's terminology. It is due to the simple fact that not every music team really worships and we cannot call worship something that it is not. Not all singing is worship and not all worship is singing.

It is clear that every band must have established operating rules, and designated hours for rehearsals. It must be harmonious and approach ministry with prayer and unity. Still, it is not a worship team but the group of musicians leading the community in worship. I have never agreed with the term nor accepted the fact that the one who is part of the worship team is a true worshiper. The Bible says: *True worshipers will worship the Father in spirit and in truth* (John 4:23, NKJV).

Jesus never mentioned anything about music. He did it on purpose because worship does not lie in music but *in Spirit and in truth*. We have twisted this image ourselves and created a substitute for worship: music. When we read about worship in the Bible, we think about music. When we hear about worship, we think about music. When we talk about worship, we talk about music. We can worship God with music, but we can also do it without it. Singing may not worship God but we may worship Him with the highest kind of worship by not singing at all.

What did Jesus want to convey about worship by saying that the hour is coming when the true worshipers will worship the Father in spirit and in truth? First of all that the time is coming when a different kind of worship will emerge. What does this mean? It means there were people who did not worship the Father in spirit and in truth. There was something wrong with their worship. Therefore, there were true and false worshipers as well as the right and the wrong ones. What determines right worship? It is the spirit and the truth. These are the values that cannot be separated. We can worship the

Father in spirit but we won't become His worshipers unless we do it in the truth. If we worship in the truth, we won't be worshipers of God unless we do it in the spirit as well. The true worshipers worship the Father in spirit and in truth. Let me explain.

We read that God is spirit in the same verse. Thus, worship must take place at the level of our spirit. Each of us is created in God's image. We are spirits, we have souls and we live in a body. We communicate with God at the spirit level. At this level, as the Bible says, we should worship God. So Jesus says this: *I want you to worship the Father not in spirit only but also in the truth.*

Spiritual matters are important to many people but they limit themselves exclusively to the realm of the spirit. This is called "spiritualization". God not only cares for the spirit, but for the soul as well. And this is the mystery of this verse. True worship lies in the spirit and soul. The truth does not dwell in our spirit but in the soul: the mind, emotions, will, desires and dreams. Therefore, God's desire is to worship Him *in spirit and in truth*. We come to the knowledge of truth when our dreams, desires and emotions are totally focused on Jesus.

We can lift our hands up, we can worship God in spirit and sing in tongues but it still does not make us true worshipers nor is it complete worship when we lack truth in our soul. God waits for those who will worship Him not only in spirit but also in truth.

When I was a teenager, a certain prophet said to me: "God smells a pleasant fragrance from you." And that was all. I completely did not understand it back then but today, when I think about it, I realize God loves our broken hearts. He loves and longs for us to offer Him a place in our hearts that up to now was occupied by something or someone else. This is the place of a pleasant fragrance for the Lord God.

A few days earlier, before I heard this sentence, the had a feeling Holy Spirit asks me a question: "Are you ready to give up something in order to know me better?" Without any hesitation I replied: "Yes, Lord". However, the following question was not as obvious to me: "Are you ready to get rid of your entire collection of music records?".

This time I did not answer without thinking or without hesitation. Music was half of my life. It was hard - very hard. I answered hesitantly after several moments: "Yes, Lord, I will do it in spite of everything". After I finished praying, I went home. Hundreds of music albums disappeared from my computer within seconds.

I could not stop crying for the next few days. Everyone at home was asking me what happened. I would sit at the table for dinner and start to eat but as soon as I thought about the recent loss, tears would start flowing. It was a very strong sensation. Why? Because the more time we devote to something, the more room in our thoughts it takes up and the more we are bound to it. And the more attached we are, the more room we give it in our hearts.

One thing is highly important in all this: God does not take away from us whatever is wrong and sinful. These are two completely different things. When we struggle with sin, we do not give our hearts to it because it is wrong. No one who is born-again wants to sin because they feel discomfort and remorse when committing a sin and they know it is wrong. Therefore, they do not give their hearts to it.

But when there is something good in our lives, we love and cherish it. We are able to give part of ourselves to it and thus taking this part away from Jesus. However, if we cherish abiding in the Holy Spirit we can be sure that God will want to take it away from us because He wants *all* of us for Himself.

In addition to the music, there were a few other things I had to give to the Lord in my life. Once, I felt strong emotions and I had to fight a serious battle with myself. God said, "This is your sacrifice". I believe there is a need of sacrifice for many people who want to know God closely and desire to be *set free* to live for Him. It is a time of dying to our greatest and most secret desires. It is a time when in one moment we need to lay down the hope for fulfilling our dreams.

God is checking whether our hearts are ready to give Him *everything*. A vessel suitable to be used by God must be empty. The Holy Spirit cannot fill vessels that are already full. Thus, we have to give *everything* to God, so that He might be *everything* for us.

I remember that evening very well. I prayed and asked God hundreds of questions: "What will happen? Are you sure? Will I make it? Do I have to? Why?" I felt like I was getting weaker and dying. I felt my soul die. My body was exhausted and my soul was empty. I gave God my most valuable things. I gave Him everything. It was a place of sacrifice, death and a pleasing fragrance to God. The feeling of emptiness within ourselves is worth paying whatever cost, for then we are sure that we have created a place for God to fill us up with Himself.

Back then God reminded me of Abraham. I literally saw him raising his hand against his son. God asked, "Are you ready to kill?" I needed the Holy Spirit to explain it to me because Abraham never really killed his son. However, we read about it twice as something that was done in the New Testament:

> By faith Abraham, when God tested him, offered Isaac as a sacrifice. He who had embraced the promises was about to sacrifice his one and only son, even though God had said to him, "It is through Isaac that your offspring will be reckoned." Abraham reasoned that God could even raise the dead, and so in a manner of speaking he did receive Isaac back from death. (Heb. 11:17-19, NKJV)

Is the Bible inaccurate here? By no means! It is very simple. The Christian God is not the God of religion but faith. It is not that the Holy Spirit loves our pain, tears and suffering. He loves our closeness, because He knows that His closeness is best thing we can have.

There is nothing in the world that would give us the true fulfillment. Often, we are anxious and struggle when we desperately want something. We dream of greatness, love, fame, power and wealth. We want to be somebody. But nothing can give us the true fulfillment. Nothing can fill the endless human desire for "something more".

Once, I played the testimony of Brian "Head" Welch at one of the youth meetings. What he talked about really struck me. I think

I got more out of this meeting than the youth. Brian talked about when he was at the top of fame. He obtained and reached it all. Millions of fans adored him, he had plenty of money and he could have had any girl he wanted – his dreams were fulfilled. And then he said: "There was nothing left in my life that I could dream about."

That was it! We often think we are happy and satisfied when our dreams come true. To our surprise, however, it turns out that it is still not that. We are still missing something. Why? Because only the Father can give us a sense of true fulfillment and satisfaction. Even the fulfillment of the most secret dreams won't do it. True fulfillment is when we are immersed in the sweet presence of the Father and His love fills every part of our being. This happens only when we become empty so that we could be filled with God. This is the most precious thing we can have in life.

Of course, we must remember that our God is not a God of set patterns but the heart. He doesn't want us to force ourselves to give Him everything we receive in this life. That is not His intention. In fact, God does not desire sacrifice but a generous heart.

This is the highest form of worship: our willingness to give God anything He asks for at any time.

In the Old Testament there was only a system based on sacrifices. In the New Covenant God wants a heart to be *ready* for sacrifice more than the sacrifice itself. The constant readiness makes a pleasant fragrance flow from our hearts to the Lord God. In Abraham's example, this is the difference between the imperfective aspect of the Old Testament and the perfect aspect in the New Testament.

Sometimes it is not easy to give up what we really love. It is the same with marriage. When a husband is doing something his wife does not like and she asks him to stop, he'll stop it without hesitation if he loves her. Love covers everything, does not seek its own and bears all things. Giving anything to God will not be a problem when we build our relationship with God based on love. It is because we know God does not want to take things from us just because he pleases to do so. The Lord takes away things because He has something *better* for us.

It is extremely important to always be ready to give Jesus His rightful place in our hearts. One of the greatest tragedies in a Christian's life is when one has nothing to give to God. In reality, however, the tragedy is not the fact that there is nothing to give to God. The worse thing is not being aware of the power that flows from the *sacrifice*.

If we realize the enormous power that lies in giving our heart to the Lord, we will never allow for not having anything that we could give to our Master.

The time for sacrifice brought one other thing into my life. God taught me that whatever we consider to be the best is merely *good* but what the Lord has for us is the *best*. That is the difference between the highest form of human goodness and the goodness of God.

Our Lord is good! Everything that comes from Him is good and focused on our well-being. However, not everything we consider good is the goodness of God. Why? Because God's goodness is higher than ours. His thoughts are not thoughts of man. His ways are not our ways. In moments like this we must trust God that He has for us something far beyond our dreams. Something that is not only good but is the *best*.

Several months after I deleted my entire music collection there were 200 original CDs on my shelf. God gave me everything back and even more. Each of us must learn this lesson. When God takes something away, He does it because He wants to have us even *closer* to Him and also, because He wants to give us something of His own, meaning something *better*. Although it often seems like nothing could be better, we must still trust, believe and remember that God's thoughts are not our thoughts.

This is what made Abraham different. Many years earlier, God gave him a promise: *Sarah shall conceive, and bear a son, and his offspring will be like the sand on the seashore.* Several years later the Lord said to him: *Give me this son, who comes from my promise.*

Where is the logic? Did it make any sense? Did God really say that? What Abraham did was extraordinary! He believed against all logic! His faith went beyond rationalism and the possibilities of the human mind! Why would God take away his son, whom He had promised him? Abraham's faith *was not a reasoning faith but a faith of the heart*. He did not think of intricate stories, he did not rationalize, he did not reason nor try to explain but he believed because he knew and trusted God. He built his faith on relationship rather than reason. Above all, we are to accept rather than understand the Word of God.

In order for God to speak to us we must listen to Him. And in order to listen to Him we must hear Him first. But we cannot hear God if we do not have time for Him. It is a simple principle. True worship of the Father results from faith and faith is formed in the place of closeness and intimacy. Therefore, there is no true listening to God without being close to Him.

In sociology, the listening process involves complete concentration on what the other person is saying. If we are not fully concentrated and are instead distracted, the hearing process is incomplete. In communication with God the listening process requires full concentration on the words we hear. However, there must be complete separation of the soul and spirit for this reason. The Bible says in Hebrews 4:12 (NKJV): *For the word of God is living and powerful, (...) piercing even to the division of soul and spirit.* Worship is the best supporting instrument in the process of separating the soul and the spirit. And music is the best instrument ushering us into this process. This is the best time to receive *spiritual and heavenly* things from the Holy Spirit. Jesus said:

> *If I have told you earthly things and you do not believe, how will you believe if I tell you heavenly things* (John 3:12, NKJV).

Jesus wants to talk to us about heavenly things but we must be ready for it. We must listen with spiritual ears and be able to communicate with the Spirit on the level of the spirit.

There is one other important element to the process of dying which needs a special place in our lives. It is fire. Each sacrifice requires fire. But what is fire?

We often say to God we need His fire but we do not think about the meaning of these words. I know the story of a man who began to shout at one church service: "Lord, I want your fire, I want your fire! Give me your fire! I want to feel it! I want to feel like I'm burning." These were strong words. The problem is that God may treat such prayer very seriously and to grant us what we ask for.

God answered the prayer of that man and gave him what he desired so much. A very difficult time began in his life. Strange things started to happen that were difficult to bear. There were serious problems, relationships conflicts with best friends, family and financial difficulties. However, it was not a result of the *fire* itself but the reaction to the fire in his life.

Fire is God's igniter for sacrifice. God sends it into our lives to burn away whatever is wrong and to destroy whatever is of us. If we are not ready for it, the results can be counterproductive.

The fire of God is not pleasant warmth but a consuming flame we feel inside. It affects all areas when it comes. It consumes everything and as it passes it leaves us transformed completely. The fire is a test. The Bible says:

> And it shall come to pass in all the land, Says the LORD, "That two-thirds in it shall be cut off and die, but one–third shall be left in it: I will bring the one–third through the fire, will refine them as silver is refined, and test them as gold is tested. They will call on my name, and I will answer them. I will say, 'This is my people'; and each one will say, 'The LORD is my God.'" (Zech 13:8-9, NKJV).

God tests our hearts much in the same way gold is refined and tested. The greatest effect and reward for passing the test of fire is the ability to recognize the time of His coming. We will always be ready to accept the fire once we know its taste. The fire is not pain or suffering sent by God but offering us the possibility to react to them. It is never physical suffering but the suffering of the soul. God desires our hearts like gold tested in the fire. The heart that has not passed the test of fire will not be ready to offer sacrifice to God.

Our strength, power and courage to offer sacrifice to God depend on the way we receive the fire. Very often this is a multi-step process that consists of several consecutive events.

The Apostle Paul said in 1 Corinthians: *I die daily* (1 Cor. 15:31, NKJV). Certainly, Paul did not mean physical death. He knew the cross that Jesus spoke about is closely connected with the death of our desires. Dying to yourself is not a demand but rather a possibility – a decision. We may decide to not give to God the desires of our hearts which He asks about, but then we won't receive anything more from Him.

There is certain limit to the knowledge of God in our lives. Our death is its limit. The more death in us, the more divine life within us. Each death is associated with our weakness. Sometimes, it is extremely difficult to carry the weight of death and that is the reason why we need the Holy Spirit. He is with us when we lack strength, when we feel a lot of pain in our souls and an excruciating cry in our hearts. He is with us in the biggest moments of weakness.

Have you ever wondered what weakness is? The Bible says:

> And He said to me, "My grace is sufficient for you, for my strength is made perfect in weakness." Therefore most gladly I will rather boast in my infirmities, that the power of Christ may rest upon me. Therefore I take pleasure in infirmities, in reproaches, in needs, in persecutions, in distresses, for Christ's sake. For when I am weak, then I am strong. (2 Cor. 12:9-10, NKJV)

Weakness is when we are too weak to say "NO" to God and strength is when we are too strong to say "YES" to God. Weakness is never in vain because God has a prize prepared for us: His power.

In closing, let's go back to the role of music in worship. Why does almost every Christian identify worship with music? Why is it often difficult to separate worship from music? The answer is very simple. Music is the best instrument to silence the soul. Maybe we never thought about it but, while singing, our mind concentrates almost entirely on the music – we keep our soul busy. That is when the space for communication with God on the spirit level is made. That is where the extraordinary secret in the power of music lies.

Therefore, we can sing with our minds but we can also sing in the spirit. We may sing beautiful songs and create music that will be nothing more than a sum of notes, melodies and chords having nothing to do with the real worship of the Father, unless it flows from the *spirit and soul.* The Bible says:

> *Surely I have calmed and quieted my soul, like a weaned child with his mother; like a weaned child is my soul within me. O Israel, hope in the* LORD *FROM this time forth and forever.* (Psalm 131:2-3, NKJV)

The fact that music is the most effective instrument to silence the soul can be seen in the Bible:

> *And Elisha said, "As the* LORD *of hosts lives, before whom I stand, surely were it not that I regard the presence of Jehoshaphat king of Judah, I would not look at you, nor see you. But now bring me a musician." Then it happened, when the musician played, that the hand of the* LORD *came upon him. And he said, "Thus says the* LORD*: 'Make this valley full of ditches.' For thus says the* LORD *... (2* Kings 3:14—17a, NKJV)

Why did Elisha ask for the music? Because he needed to silence his soul in order to concentrate on what God was saying. Music is a great instrument to silence the soul. It allows worshiping the Father in freedom whereas silencing of the soul is the best method to experience intimacy with God - to communicate with Him.

It is similar with loud expressions of praise to God. We remember what happened when one hundred and twenty trumpeters, choristers and singers sang a song of praise to God together on the occasion of bringing the ark of covenant into the temple erected by Solomon[23]. Similarly, great things took place when Paul and Silas sang loudly for God in prison. There is enormous power in music. When combined with faith, incredible and inconceivable things happen. God cannot ignore the sound coming from a heart in sincere worship of Him.

In my life, music helped me in almost every prayer to separate daily issues from my heart by crying to the Lord in longing and love. Therefore, music is a precious gift given to us by the Lord.

We can worship the Father during Sunday service, raise hands to Him and sing beautiful Christian songs. There is nothing wrong with it. But we can also do more: offer God a sweet fragrance of sacrifice – the scent of death as the greatest expression of worship. This is what opens the gates of the heavenly courtroom before us.

The next chapter is about the power of God. We all know that God has power. We also know that He is a powerful and omnipotent God. However, seldom do we think about what the power of God really is and what role it plays in our daily lives. Also, I will share about some events from my life when the power of God became difficult to bear for me.

---

[23] 2 Chron. 5:12-14

Prayer

(*Lyrics*: Terry MacAlmon, Holy Are You Lord)

Can you hear the sound of heaven
Like the sound of many waters
It's the sound of worship coming from the throne
There are cries of adoration
As men from every nation
Lift their voice to make His glory known, singing

Holy, holy, holy are You, Lord
Holy, holy, holy are You, Lord

THINK IT OVER ONE MORE TIME

➤ *What is the difference* between worship and music? Is all music worship? Is all worship music?

➤ What does it mean to worship the Father in spirit and in truth?

➤ Are you ready to give God everything He asks for? Is there anything within yourself that you are ready to put to death?

➤ How do you see the difference between your goodness and the goodness of God? Explain.

➤ Is it possible for God to smell a pleasing fragrance from you? Do you desire it? What are the steps you intend to take to do this?

Then Jacob was left alone; and a Man wrestled with him until the breaking of day. Now when He saw that He did not prevail against him, He touched the socket of his hip; and the socket of Jacob's hip was out of joint as He wrestled with him. And He said, "Let Me go, for the day breaks." But he said, "I will not let You go unless You bless me!" So He said to him, "What is your name?" He said, "Jacob." And He said, "Your name shall no longer be called Jacob, but Israel; for you have struggled with God and with men, and have prevailed." Then Jacob asked, saying, "Tell me Your name, I pray." And He said, "Why is it that you ask about My name?" And He blessed him there. So Jacob called the name of the place Peniel: "For I have seen God face to face, and my life is preserved." Just as he crossed over Penuel the sun rose on him, and he limped on his hip.

(Gen. *32:24-31*, NKJV)

10

THE REALITY OF THE POWER OF GOD

*The power of God is a spiritual substance – it penetrates
the entire being as it touches the spirit, soul and body.*

The power of God is a particularly sensitive issue for the
Church. Some treat it as a "virtual" attribute of God. Others
see it as a generally understood power. Still others see it as
something tangible and real. The problem is that there is not just one
definition of God's power in the Bible.

The fact is that as Christians, we have an excessive tendency to
generalize and unify terms used in church. We often confuse them
and ascribe the same meaning to different terms. First of all, this leads
to unnecessary aversion toward those who believe differently and also
limits our knowledge of God in a new and personal dimension. If we
only know one out of many aspects of the power of God, we will
limit our lives to experiencing God's power just in the dimension
we know or we won't experience it at all.

The Word of God reveals to us many dimensions of the power
of God. The Bible does not only speak about the power of creation,
reign or protection but also about the power of healing, touching
and transforming our soul and body.

First of all, the omnipotence of God has to be clearly established.

It is the highest form of power in the universe that cannot be seen or understood in individual or human terms. The Bible says:

His glory covered the heavens, and the earth was full of His praise. His brightness was like the light; He had rays flashing from His hand, and there His power was hidden. Before Him went pestilence, and fever followed at His feet. He stood and measured the earth; He looked and startled the nations. And the everlasting mountains were scattered, the perpetual hills bowed. His ways are everlasting. (Hab. 3:3-6, NKJV)

Is this not a scary image? But is there anything that is not true? Not at all. However, God does not use this power toward man because the entire human race would be lost in just a moment if it were so. Regardless, it is interesting how clearly we, as Christians, perceive the power of God in only one dimension - as an inaccessible, omnipotent power that is distant and alien to man.

We can read many times in the Bible about the power of God as a potential being expressed in a readiness to act and to exercise power. God's power is permanent, independent, sovereign and unfathomable. All power and all authority belong to God.

God has spoken once, twice I have heard this: that power belongs to God. (Ps. 62:11, NKJV)

By His Spirit He adorned the heavens; His hand pierced the fleeing serpent. Indeed these are the mere edges of His ways, and how small a whisper we hear of Him! But the thunder of His power who can understand? (Job 26:13-14, NKJV)

God is immense in His power. He does great things and moves mountains but ... it does not concern me. Such attitude is one of the biggest mistakes in our personal lives with the Holy Spirit. God did not limit his power only to the vast potency that no one will ever be able to comprehend. There is no doubt about the fact that God is omnipotent and omniscient, yet He functions with us on a level we can access. And this truth should be the most important for us. Our Lord is not only a great and awesome God but He is a close and understanding Father also.

The devil really wants Christians to believe that God's power is only a feature attributed to God to which we don't need to give any special attention. It would be best if we agreed and accepted it as a permanent order of things and for us not to need the power of God in our daily lives. This happens in the Church very often but in my personal life it was completely different. God not only let me know of His power and taught me of its availability but He would hit me with it just as often as He did with Jacob. This issue seems a bit touchy and delicate because the Old Testament stories are usually perceived figuratively without treating many things literally.

Jacob's story is somewhat different. Jacob fought and wrestled with God. Of course, it was not a fight to the death. It was all about the blessing. Jacob is a symbol of a person determined and ready to do whatever it takes in order to have as much as possible from God.

God's attitude towards Jacob is very encouraging. In spite of Jacob's inappropriate methods, God acknowledged his heart hungry for blessings. Our Father likes it when our hearts are desperate to know Him. From a human perspective, some methods may seem to be highly inappropriate, but to God, our desire is what matters more. Jacob's desire was tremendous. First of all, he deceived his father to get a blessing but he did not stop there. He wanted something more! He started to fight God Himself.

If God had wanted, he could have killed Jacob in a moment. But He functions with us on a level accessible for us. How is it possible then for Jacob to fight with God? Well, God did not wrestle with him physically but spiritually. Such struggle is not measured by the capability of flesh but by the potential of our spirit.

I also had such prayers in my life when I *wrestled* with God. Certainly the struggle was not the same as with Jacob's struggle but I also felt God *strike* me. The Bible does not speak of the Jacob's struggle as something symbolic. Jacob did fight and wrestle with God and, therefore, each of us can do it too. This is good news for everyone.

Our Father does not give away His gifts and blessings randomly. He is waiting for those who will catch Him and won't let go just like Jacob did. It lasted all night until morning, but God finally gave Jacob what he desired - He blessed him. How many of us need a blessing today? Let us, therefore, cease to pray with a pleading voice, grab a hold of God and don't let go until we get what we desire.

I remember a few years ago during one of the evening prayers I shouted to God that I want more from Him. And then it all started. I fell down. I tried to get back up, but then again, "boom" - I fell again. I fell under the power of prayer many times before but this experience was different. I felt like God was hitting me. I was trying to get back up but God would literally knock me down with His power as though I was a bag. It was very strong and intense. I did not fall down because I was weak but it felt like "something" would literally knock or throw me down to the ground. At one point I said, "Lord, that is enough. Please do not kill me."

How is it possible for things like that to happen in our lives? It is because the power of God is a spiritual substance that penetrates the entire being and affects the spirit, soul and body. So it was with me then. I felt like a spiritual substance penetrated me. The room I was in was empty and yet "something" would literally knock me to the ground. This "something" was the power of God. The Bible says:

> *Now a woman, having a flow of blood for twelve years, who had spent all her livelihood on physicians and could not be healed by any, came from behind and touched the border of His garment. And immediately her flow of blood stopped. And Jesus said, "Who touched Me?" When all denied it, Peter and those with him said, "Master, the multitudes throng and press You, and You say, 'Who touched Me?'" But Jesus said, "Somebody touched Me, for I perceived power going out from Me." Now when the woman saw that*

she was not hidden, she came trembling; and falling down before Him, she declared to Him in the presence of all the people the reason she had touched Him and how she was healed immediately. And He said to her, "Daughter, be of good cheer; your faith has made you well. Go in peace." (Luke 8:43-48, NKJV)

I love reading this. Here within lie many great revelations. However, for me what attracts the most attention are the words of Jesus to His disciples: *Somebody touched Me, for I perceived power going out from Me.*

Power left Jesus. Thus it is something real and true. It is true that the power of God is a spiritual substance – something that comes out, moves, what that can penetrate, touch and knock us to the ground.

In another place the Bible says:

Now it happened on a certain day, as He was teaching, that there were Pharisees and teachers of the law sitting by, who had come out of every town of Galilee, Judea, and Jerusalem. And the power of the Lord was present to heal them. (Luke 5:17, NKJV)

The power of Jesus always has a specific goal. When it goes out and touches us, it happens for a reason. This is why it is so important for us to desire it. The Bible says the Lord's power to heal was in Jesus. This phrase does not mean the power to heal the sick only. Today, Jesus also uses His power to heal our wounded souls. It is a wonderful biblical truth. Jesus is not only a physician of our flesh but also of our souls.

How can one enter the place of God's power? The answer is found in the book of Isaiah:

For thus says the Lord God, the Holy One of Israel: "In returning and rest you shall be saved; In quietness and confidence shall be your strength." (Isaiah 10:15, NKJV)

The power of God comes from quietness and confidence. Quietness is the best place for our soul where we can open ourselves to the flow of the power of God. It does not say anything about the silence of the flesh but of the calming of the soul. We need to separate these two. Sometimes the cry of the body causes greater quietness in our soul than silence. I spent several years in searching, asking, screaming and constant crying before I started to feel the power of God. After a few years, God opened for me the door to His power. Power was born in quietness and confidence.

How does one release the power of God? Do it in the name of Jesus. Again, I recall one of my prayers when I told God that I wanted to check it out. The Holy Spirit told me, "Try to use the name of Jesus." And then I started to say "Jesus"! Each time I said it, I fell to the ground - *something* would knock me down. It really worked!

Many Christians have a problem with understanding the issue of falling down under the power of God. Where does the doubt come from? It is due to limiting God to the confines set by our mind.

Religion puts the ways of God into our own way of doing things as well as limits the Holy Spirit to certain rhetoric and boxes. Religiosity results from the lack of intimacy and the lack of divine life flowing through us. All the walls are torn down and all the limits are destroyed when we enter into the depth of relationship with the Holy Spirit because we get to know God as Father rather than as a set of certain standards or ideas. We get to know Him as a real Person - the creator of man. That is when we cease to operate according to our own *understanding* and we do not try to understand everything at all costs. We accept it rather as a natural fruit of God's work, resulting from a *relationship* based on love.

We can find several passages in the Word of God that very clearly describe the phenomenon of falling under the influence of God's power:

> *Jesus therefore, knowing all things that would come upon Him, went forward and said to them, "Whom are you seeking?" They answered Him, "Jesus of Nazareth." Jesus said to them,*

"I am He." And Judas, who betrayed Him, also stood with them. Now when He said to them, "I am He," they drew back and fell to the ground. (John 18:4-6, NKJV)

I, John, both your brother and companion in the tribulation and kingdom and patience of Jesus Christ, was on the island that is called Patmos for the word of God and for the testimony of Jesus Christ. I was in the Spirit on the Lord's Day, and I heard behind me a loud voice, as of a trumpet, saying, "I am the Alpha and the Omega, the First and the Last," and, "What you see, write in a book and send it to the seven churches which are in Asia: to Ephesus, to Smyrna, to Pergamos, to Thyatira, to Sardis, to Philadelphia, and to Laodicea." Then I turned to see the voice that spoke with me. And having turned I saw seven golden lampstands, and in the midst of the seven lampstands One like the Son of Man, clothed with a garment down to the feet and girded about the chest with a golden band. His head and hair were white like wool, as white as snow, and His eyes like a flame of fire; His feet were like fine brass, as if refined in a furnace, and His voice as the sound of many waters; He had in His right hand seven stars, out of His mouth went a sharp two-edged sword, and His countenance was like the sun shining in its strength. And when I saw Him, I fell at His feet as dead. But He laid His right hand on me, saying to me, "Do not be afraid; I am the First and the Last. I am He who lives, and was dead, and behold, I am alive forevermore. Amen. And I have the keys of Hades and of Death. (Rev. 1:9-18, NKJV)

But He laid His right hand on me, saying to me, "Do not be afraid!" Jesus always does that. His touch always brings peace. His power brings faith and courage, and His arms constantly silence our souls!

I am not in favor of the rational persuasion that being "slain in the Spirit" or "falling down under the power" is good and biblically correct. It does not make any sense at this point. If we do not enter into a place of intimacy with God, if we do not invite the Holy Spirit into our lives and allow for His life to flow in us, we'll never know the true taste of the power of God. It is not a matter of belief but of personal experience. We can go to different conferences and do interviews with people. We can try to study and describe it. We can connect people to different devices in order to examine their brain activity and heart rate. Yet still it is not going to explain anything to us.

A few years ago I read a book on laughter in the Holy Spirit. While reading, just one thing made me wonder: Has the author ever laughed in the Holy Spirit? It turned out that she had not. However, at all costs, she tried to study this phenomenon at an intellectual level. It looked like a man trying to understand with all his strength the experience of giving birth. He could even write his doctoral dissertation on this, but unless he experiences it, his arguments will still only remain a theory.

However, what puzzles me the most is the fact that the author never even interviewed a person who experienced laughter in the Holy Spirit. The reason I wonder about it is because the *origin* and the feelings that accompany such manifestations are more important than only the external expressions. There is nothing wrong with them if they result from communion with the Holy Spirit.

I was never taught about these things in my life. No one ever explained them to me. As a teenager, I did not know the doctrines of other religions either. I believed God and I loved my Father. I met Him as my Daddy and I started to experience His miraculous touch.

One thing is sure: each of us is different and we cannot demand from others the same things God gives to us. The Holy Spirit does not have a fixed plan of action in relationships with us. He talks and touches each person differently. This is due to the simple fact that we all have a different personality, expressiveness and sensitivity. Therefore, let's not try to explain what we don't know only at the level of the mind.

Life with God is not a rational tour of intellectual trails. God cannot be known by the mind. For what is our mind to be able to comprehend the Creator of the universe?

Blaise Pascal, a French scientist, mathematician and philosopher said: *The evidence of God's existence and his gift is more than compelling, but those who insist that they have no need of him, or it, will always find ways to discount the offer.* It is the same with the power of God – there will always be people who will find ways to despise it. Therefore, it is vain to argue and persuade that it is good. The power of God is not a toy but a real thing and is not born outside of a place of intimacy with the Holy Spirit.

The power of God is not virtual but is very real in character. God gave us His power so that we could base our faith on it. The Bible says:

> For I determined not to know anything among you except Jesus Christ and Him crucified. I was with you in weakness, in fear, and in much trembling. And my speech and my preaching were not with persuasive words of human wisdom, but in demonstration of the Spirit and of power, that your faith should not be in the wisdom of men but in the power of God. (1 Cor. 2:2-5, NKJV)

We can hear many sermons and testimonies preached with "persuasive words of human wisdom" and full of lofty ideas and thorough interpretation of Bible passages. However, the Bible says we are to base our faith on *power*. Thus, we need the Spirit and the power that confirms the Word.

It is a wonderful and amazing truth. God did not only leave words with us but He gave us the Holy Spirit and His power. Therefore, we can be sure that when the power of the Holy Spirit descends upon us, it is what we can *base* our faith upon. It is inappropriate though to limit the power of God to only the anointing flowing *through* us. The Lord wants the power to be *in* us as well as *for* us. It will be power for our faith.

I remember many instances when the power of the Holy Spirit descended upon me in strange circumstances. Several times I fell suddenly under the power of the Holy Spirit while in an elevator. At other times it happened while I was talking on the phone or while walking. There was always a purpose to it. Each time the Lord touches us He desires to change us, draw our attention to something or help us to listen to His voice. Therefore, the power of God is what the Lord desires for anyone ready to accept it. Are you ready?

Prayer

(Lyrics: Vineyard, Surrender)

I'm giving You my heart, all that is within
I lay it all down, for the sake of You my King

I'm giving You my dreams, laying down my rights
I'm giving up my pride, for the promise of new life

AND I SURRENDER ALL TO YOU, ALL TO YOU
AND I SURRENDER ALL TO YOU, ALL TO YOU

THINK IT OVER ONE MORE TIME

> ➤ *What are the* types of divine power? How is it possible for the power of God to be available to man?

> ➤ What can we learn from Jacob's wrestling with God?

> ➤ Have you ever wrestled with God?

> ➤ What can you say about the quietness that flows from the power of God?

> ➤ Do you desire the power of God in your life?

After these things I looked, and behold, a door standing open in heaven. And the first voice which I heard was like a trumpet speaking with me, saying, "Come up here, and I will show you things which must take place after this." Immediately I was in the Spirit; and behold, a throne set in heaven, and One sat on the throne.

(Rev. 4:1–2, NKJV)

11

THE GLORY OF HEAVEN

*Everything, even the greatest pleasure of this world is nothing
compared to the glory of the world where we belong.*

I t was very late. Slowly, the night was approaching and I was still
down on the church floor barely moving. I was overcome by
the glory of God. I was experiencing heaven.

I couldn't get over the fact that I had to get back to my regular
life. Whenever I tried to get up, the tears would flow down from my
eyes themselves and I would fall down on the ground again. I could
not stand the fact that I had to remain in the world rather than to be
with the Lord and stay in His house forever. I remember crying, *Lord,
kill me, please. I want to be with you now!* My flesh barely withstood
it – it tussled as though the spirit wanted to get rid of it forever. And
God came down to me with His glory and let me taste heaven right
there for the first time.

On that very day Holy Spirit reminded me His words: *Eye has
not seen, nor ear heard, nor have entered into the heart of man. The things
which God has prepared for those who love Him. But God has revealed them
to us through His Spirit.* (1 Corinthians 2:9-10). In this way God says
He gives us the opportunity to feel the atmosphere of heaven here
on earth. And this is what happened in my case.

I do not remember anyone teaching on this passage from the Word of God in relation to the present. Usually, it is said that whatever God has prepared for us in heaven is so wonderful, that no ear has heard, no eye has seen nor has it even entered into the heart of man. However, the truth we learn from these words is about something else: God has prepared great things for all those who love Him, but He revealed them (*to us*) already here on earth!

The conclusion is very simple. We will all make it to heaven someday and we will hear what no human ear has heard and no human eye has seen. We can accept it, rejoice about it and wait for heaven after death. But we can have it today! It entirely depends on us.

The glory cannot be described in human words. It cannot be comprehended with the human mind and our human bodies cannot contain it. The glory comes from the invisible world – from the heavenly world.

God allows us to feel the actual atmosphere of heaven when the glory of God descends upon us. In other words, the glory is the presence of heaven. It is the heavy presence of God Himself. When we collide with it, we immediately notice the imperfections and finiteness of the world and we realize that the flesh is only a kind of tent that we need in order to live on earth. In one moment we become aware that the real us is not the flesh but the spirit. We see a big difference between the visible and the invisible world. Although the glory of heaven is real, it cannot remain with us forever because we would have to die – leave our body. In fact, our bodies are too imperfect in order to continually contain the glory of God.

God gives us a taste of heaven so that we would know that we are destined for a different world and that the Lord has placed eternity in us. The Holy Spirit does it so we can realize that the world we live in is only a short journey to be completed in eternity.

My entire value system completely changed within few moments of my colliding with the glory of heaven. The worldly pleasures I have known till now have lost their glitter, become pale and devoid of any flavor. Nothing except the Lord mattered to me at that moment. I only wanted to be with Him. Everything else lost its sense because even the greatest thing of this world fades away when compared to the glory of God.

Back then I was reminded of the lyrics of an old hymn. Previously, they were only words to me but now they have become a revelation:

> *Turn your eyes upon Jesus; Look full in His wonderful face;*
> *And the things of earth will grow strangely dim; In the light*
> *of His glory and grace.*

Sometimes we do not think about the true meaning of words while singing Christian songs. Earlier, this hymn seemed to be only a nice and unspecified group of words to me. But they became an accurate reflection of my heart's condition when I collided with heaven. Everything started to become strangely alien and distant to me. The Bible says:

> *For I consider that the sufferings of this present time are not worthy to be compared with the glory which shall be revealed in us. For the earnest expectation of the creation eagerly waits for the revealing of the sons of God. For the creation was subjected to futility, not willingly, but because of Him who subjected it in hope; because the creation itself also will be delivered from the bondage of corruption into the glorious liberty of the children of God.* (Romans 8:18-21, NKJV)

> *For we know that if our earthly house, this tent, is destroyed, we have a building from God, a house not made with hands, eternal in the heavens. For in this we groan, earnestly desiring to be clothed with our habitation which is from heaven, if indeed, having been clothed, we shall not be found naked. For we who are in this tent groan, being burdened, not because we want to be unclothed, but further clothed, that mortality may be swallowed up by life. Now He who has prepared us for this very thing is God, who also has given us the Spirit as a guarantee. So we are always confident,*

knowing that while we are at home in the body we are
absent from the Lord. For we walk by faith, not by sight.
We are confident, yes, well pleased rather to be absent from
the body and to be present with the Lord. (Romans 8:18–
21, NKJV)

There is one thought that clearly emerges from the above-mentioned passages: our bodies are passing away, imperfect, subject to the bondage of corruption and mortal. But the Lord says there is a day coming when whatever is mortal will be swallowed up by everlasting life.

We have received the Holy Spirit as a guarantee of the life-to-come. Paul had this revealed to him. He very often mentioned that we are away from the Lord as long as we live in the flesh. It was the longing of his heart and the biggest dilemma of his life. He said:

For to me, to live is Christ, and to die is gain. But if I live
on in the flesh, this will mean fruit from my labor; yet what
I shall choose I cannot tell. For I am hard-pressed between
the two, having a desire to depart and be with Christ, which
is far better. (Phil. 1:21-23, NKJV)

I think that only few would have the courage to publicly say that death is gain for them. Only those who have a revelation of heaven and eternity can say it.

There is a difference between knowledge and revelation that determines our behavior and decisions – it changes our lifestyle. Death is the gain because we will no longer remain in the corrupted and imperfect flesh but we will be clothed with immortality.

I remember when I was a teenager I was very afraid of the fact that while in heaven we may still sin as Lucifer did, be cast down and condemned to eternal damnation. I could not understand why we were to go to heaven since there is a probability throughout eternity of a moment of weakness. How great was my joy when I read the passage one day that dispelled my doubts:

Behold, I tell you a mystery: We shall not all sleep, but we shall all be changed - in a moment, in the twinkling of an eye, at the last trumpet. For the trumpet will sound, and the dead will be raised incorruptible, and we shall be changed. For this corruptible must put on incorruption, and this mortal must put on immortality. So when this corruptible has put on incorruption, and this mortal has put on immortality, then shall be brought to pass the saying that is written: "Death is swallowed up in victory." (1 Cor. 15:51-54, NKJV)

In the book of Revelation we read that there will be no more death, for the former things have passed away. There is only life awaiting us in eternity and our bodies will not have a single particle of death in them.

The cult of the flesh created by the media will not change the situation - the flesh is still subject to the bondage of corruption. We grow old and the cells in our bodies die every day. We are destined to die. However, there will come a day when we will receive new bodies and we'll be clothed with immortality. We will never die again and our bodies will be glorified like Jesus when He was glorified. The passage illustrating heavenly bodies is in the Gospel of John.

Now Thomas, called the Twin, one of the twelve, was not with them when Jesus came. The other disciples therefore said to him, "We have seen the Lord." So he said to them, "Unless I see in His hands the print of the nails, and put my finger into the print of the nails, and put my hand into His side, I will not believe." And after eight days His disciples were again inside, and Thomas with them. Jesus came, the doors being shut, and stood in the midst, and said, "Peace to you!" (John 20:24-26, NKJV)

This is neither logical nor possible from the Greek[24] point of view. However, the spiritual world does not exist in order to be

---

[24] Humanistic.

comprehended by the mind. Glorified bodies operate in the realm of the spirit. They are no longer surrounded by natural, imperfect and corrupted tissue, but they are spiritual, perfect and immortal bodies. Jesus entered a room despite the closed door and after a moment Thomas could place his hand in the real body of Jesus. Where is the logic in this? Let us remember that the Bible is not based on logic, but on the revelation of an infinite person of God.

Not everything can be explained by the mind because the spiritual world and its rules go beyond the capabilities of understanding in the physical world.

When our Lord comes to us in His glory, we have an impression as if flooded by an ocean of fire and love, something completely out of this world. We sense a huge weight, which despite the unprecedented burden, is the sweetest thing we can imagine. That is the atmosphere of heaven and the heavenly place of worship described in the book of Revelation.

After these things I looked, and behold, a door standing open in heaven. And the first voice which I heard was like a trumpet speaking with me, saying, "Come up here, and I will show you things which must take place after this." Immediately I was in the Spirit; and behold, a throne set in heaven, and One sat on the throne.

The four living creatures, each having six wings, were full of eyes around and within. And they do not rest day or night, saying: "Holy, holy, holy, Lord God Almighty, Who was and is and is to come!" Whenever the living creatures give glory and honor and thanks to Him who sits on the throne, who lives forever and ever, the twenty-four elders fall down before Him who sits on the throne and worship Him who lives forever and ever, and cast their crowns before the throne, saying: "You are worthy, O Lord, to receive glory and honor and power; For You created all things, and by Your will they exist and were created." (Rev. 4: 1-2, 8-12, NKJV)

The Apostle John saw heaven and experienced its atmosphere. Sometimes we wonder what the singing of *Holy, holy, holy* will involve. What is so exciting about it to do it constantly? This is due to the lack of experience of the manifested presence of God. The glory of heaven can change it in a moment.

Heaven is a place where we can fully experience God's presence and glory - a place where we are deprived of *everything* which can hinder us in doing so.

During one of my encounters with God, when the glory came down upon me once again in such a tangible manner that the world seemed to be strange and distant to me, I knew right then what the singing of *holy, holy, holy* is about. I could sing this forever, remain in that place and never leave. The spiritual pleasures I experienced then cannot be compared with any other temporary pleasures I had before because they came from the invisible world - the world of the heavens.

Almost everyone has a tendency to search for attractions and pleasures. That is natural. The problem is we often only understand them in terms of the flesh. We imagine singing and worship as something physical and so we perceive them through the prism of the flesh.

When I organized a joint trip a few years ago as the leader of the youth group, many people asked me what attractions I expected. It was a sightseeing trip and I did not plan any attractions other than admiring the beauty of nature and the building of relationships.

This is who we are – we look for excitement in almost everything. Unfortunately, the glory of God will never provide it. It is because it goes beyond the cognitive abilities of our flesh. It is the place prepared for the spirit. Unless we learn how to be sensitive and open to the Holy Spirit (and this is only done through relationship based on intimacy, closeness and trust), we will never know this place and until the end of our days on earth we'll wonder what lies behind singing: *Holy, holy, holy.*

One of the biggest tragedies in the Christian life is to leave this world without knowing the world to which you are going. Without being aware of what the eternity is, we are stripped of the power to fight for *it*. It is hard to fight for something we do not know. It is difficult to realize the value of spiritual reward we fight for in the real world when we do not know the world of the heavens.

We read in the book of Revelation that *behold, a door standing open in heaven and One sat on the throne* ... The Holy Spirit wants everyone to know this place - the place from where you can see heaven's door wide open and the Lord is sitting on a throne.

The above text implies that in the beginning, John didn't know whom the person was sitting on the throne. However, the last verses of this chapter indicate that John knows that person very well: *You are worthy, O Lord, to receive glory and honor and power.* It happened! This was accomplished through the touch of the glory of God - the revelation of the holiness of God.

The singing of: *Holy, holy, holy,* is not about pronouncing words which mean little to us - this is worship flowing from the knowledge of Jesus Christ. Holiness is the personification of God's nature. The singing of: *Holy, holy, holy* means understanding the difference between corruption of earth and the perfection of heaven. In the Book of Isaiah we read similar words:

> "For behold, I create new heavens and a new earth. And
> the former shall not be remembered or come to mind. But
> be glad and rejoice forever in what I create; for behold,
> I create Jerusalem as a rejoicing, and her people a joy.
> (Isa 65:17–18, NKJV)

God told Isaiah that when a person touches heaven, he will no longer remember the old things and they will not come to his mind. Why? It is because he will be glad and rejoice over the presence of the Lord in the New Jerusalem.

Sometimes we wonder if we will remember in heaven what happened on the earth. Will the ancient mysteries find explanation, or will we be able to check on what intrigued us earlier. God says we will forget these things and we will not recall them anymore. We will rather be fascinated by the beauty and wonder of the Lord.

Another unusual discovery coming from the knowledge of God's glory is the ability to enter a place of intimacy on the spirit level. I remember one time when God came to me again with His glory and the Holy Spirit reminded me of another passage from the Word of God:

> *Do you not know that your bodies are members of Christ? Shall I then take the members of Christ and make them members of a harlot? Certainly not! Or do you not know that he who is joined to a harlot is one body with her? For "the two," He says, "shall become one flesh." But he who is joined to the Lord is one spirit with Him.* (1 Cor. 6:51-17, NKJV)

I was shocked. I experienced one of the greatest discoveries of my Christian life in a single moment. It may seem a bit odd and incomprehensible but that is exactly what the Bible says: you can become one with another person in the flesh but you can also become one with God in the Spirit. The extraordinary burden of revelation underlies in it.

What is this passage really about? The Lord gives us a comparison of the highest relation of flesh and spirit. Flesh can unite with flesh but it will never be a complete unity. It is only the unity of the flesh. On the other hand, the one who unites with the Lord becomes one with Him in spirit.

Closeness and intimacy is limited at the level of the flesh because if we wanted to become one with someone in body and soul, we would have to mix each other's blood and have a single mind, which is impossible. So relationships between human beings is very limited but a relationship with the Lord goes beyond the knowledge of the flesh and soul. It is a spirit-to-spirit relationship: *But he who is joined to the Lord is one spirit with Him.* A relationship with God is something greater and more beautiful. The most crucial moment of intimacy is in the place of experiencing the glory of God; the connection of the human spirit with the Holy Spirit.

Marriage is a beautiful image of the relationship with God because we can also encounter Him in a place of intimacy reserved only for us. It is a place of closeness to the glory of God; the courtyard of heaven. Can we compare a fleshly and temporary closeness to the intimacy with the Lord Himself and unity of flesh to the unity of spirit? Never. This image is very clear. The Word of God is precise. In a sexual act one can be joined with another person, but in the spirit, unity can be achieved with the Lord! When we connect with the spiritual world of heaven, the glory of God covers us.

What is glory? How can we define it? First of all, we must clearly state that glory cannot be separated from God. By saying, "the glory descended upon me" we cannot say that "something" touched us. The glory does not touch us but covers, fills and overwhelms us.

The glory is being one with God. It is the tangible and manifested presence of *heaven*. It is the full expression and manifestation of the person of God. It brings God's holiness and love, as well as, a sweetness of His presence.

I would like to clarify something at this point. There is a common idea in Christianity stating that holiness is difficult to achieve. It has something to do with morality, ethics or observance of religious rituals. However, a true and godly type of holiness is the condition of the heart, which is unified with a perfect and loving world of heaven. Holiness is not something that can be achieved. Holiness is seeing the world through the eyes of God.

When we think about glory and power, both terms seem to be similar and difficult to distinguish. The Lord taught me the difference between them and showed this to me very clearly in His Word. Glory *descends* upon us or *covers us* and power *touches* us or *comes out* of us.

The power of the Lord always comes with a specific purpose. The Bible talks about the power of the Lord to heal. It also says that power "overshadowed Mary", it "had gone out of Jesus" and "power comes out" of the hands of the Lord. Power appears for us to perform a specific task. On the other hand, glory descends upon us or covers us for God's tangible presence of heaven to be manifested.

Glory comes in order to experience a close encounter with God – it is a link between the natural and supernatural. It is literally a portion of heaven!

In the Word of God, we see the glory of God appearing most often during worship or sacrifice. God came with such tangible and intense glory that human flesh could not withstand it and would fall to the ground. They would yield to the enormous strength and might of the revelation of the person of God. So it was with the tabernacle of Moses, the Temple of Solomon, the story of Ezekiel and many other stories described in the Scriptures.

In Revelation we read about the separation of glory from power: *The temple was filled with smoke from the glory of God and from His power, and no one was able to enter the temple till the seven plagues of the seven angels were completed.* (Rev. 15:8, NKJV) When the glory comes, we do not say that God sent His glory but rather that God *has come in His glory.* The difference here is crucial because the glory cannot be separated from God. The glory is not a selective attribute of God but a full revelation of the person of God. In contrast, the power of God is a force - a spiritual substance, ready to touch, change, heal and perform the supernatural. It is a constantly awaiting supernatural potential aimed to perform. Exactly like dynamite ready to explode when the fuse is lighted.

There is a passage in 2 Chronicles that is often cited regarding spiritual rebirth and revival. I have never heard anybody preach about it in the context of power is dependent on glory.

> *Also the Levites which were the singers, all of them of Asaph, of Heman, of Jeduthun, with their sons and their brethren, being arrayed in white linen, having cymbals and psalteries and harps, stood at the east end of the altar, and with them an hundred and twenty priests sounding with trumpets:) It came even to pass, as the trumpeters and singers were as one, to make one sound to be heard in praising and thanking the*

Lord; and when they lifted up their voice with the trumpets and cymbals and instruments of musick, and praised the Lord, saying, For he is good; for his mercy endureth for ever: that then the house was filled with a cloud, even the house of the Lord; So that the priests could not stand to minister by reason of the cloud: for the glory of the Lord had filled the house of God. (2 Chronicles 5:12-14, KJV)

We see an obvious dependence here. It is not the glory that flows from power but the power flows from the glory. The power of God cannot be known without knowing God's glory! The priests only fell when they encountered the glory of the Lord. Only then did the power of God manifest itself. This passage explains a lot to us. We shouldn't seek the power of God without desiring the glory of God. It will never work. Let's seek the glory of God first, let's embrace it, and then God will send His power. Without intimacy we won't know the power of God. And it is something wonderful!

Many Christians look for power today - something spectacular, great and tangible. Something they could show off, present themselves with and with it, stand out from others. But the Bible says that dependence is quite different. First, let's seek the Lord's heart - the place of glory. Let's desire to enter into a relationship with Him based on intimacy and trust. And then God will send the power. It will be a natural consequence of our relationship with Him. This is the true biblical way to know the power of God.

How can we enter this place? The Apostle Paul says we have this treasure in earthen vessels that the excellence of power may be of God and not of us. This verse very clearly indicates the source of God's power. It only flows from the Spirit of God. The flesh has nothing to do with it because it is imperfect and corrupted.

The only possible way to experience God's glory and power is by the spirit. Despite appearances, it is not difficult. The more flesh in us, the less spirit we have. The more spirit, the less flesh. Our life is a decision whether we want to live in the realm of the flesh and be very limited in the awareness of the spiritual realm – which is the one our Lord moves in. Or maybe we want to enter into a relationship with the Lord on the spiritual level. This is a decision of the heart.

I love teaching about being hungry for God. That it is the key factor here. When we are thirsty and hungry for the things of God, our life begins to be determined by the hunger of knowing the glory of God because that is when we will do anything to satisfy that hunger. We are ready to pay any price! Hunger triggers action.

Before the Lord came to me with the glory of heaven, I desired Him; I sought, knocked and yelled. When I tasted the glory, there was nothing else I wanted. I got to know everything and I could die.

The Bible says that no one has ever seen the Father and cannot see Him, however, He has revealed Himself to us through the spirit. The passage from 2 Corinthians perfectly describes this dependence.

> *For our light affliction, which is but for a moment, is working for us a far more exceeding and eternal weight of glory, while we do not look at the things which are seen, but at the things which are not seen. For the things which are seen are temporary, but the things which are not seen are eternal* (2 Cor. 4:17-18, NKJV).

Eternity lies in the realm of the spirit and we can only experience the glory of God in that place. There is no mystery about it. The more time we spend with the Lord, the more we are aware of the invisible and spiritual realm.

I have experienced the glory of God in my life several times. These moments were out of this world. I very clearly felt the gap between the realm of the spirit and flesh. I also very clearly felt the difference between the imperfection and transience of flesh, as well as, the perfection and eternity of the spirit. I tasted heaven.

In the Old Testament we read that Moses could not enter the tabernacle because the place was filled with the glory of the Lord. In the New Testament we read something completely different:

*And we have such trust through Christ toward God. Not
that we are sufficient of ourselves to think of anything as
being from ourselves, but our sufficiency is from God, who
also made us sufficient as ministers of the new covenant,
not of the letter but of the Spirit; for the letter kills, but the
Spirit gives life. But if the ministry of death, written and
engraved on stones, was glorious, so that the children of
Israel could not look steadily at the face of Moses because of
the glory of his countenance, which glory was passing away,
how will the ministry of the Spirit not be more glorious? For
if the ministry of condemnation had glory, the ministry of
righteousness exceeds much more in glory. For even what was
made glorious had no glory in this respect, because of the glory
that excels. For if what is passing away was glorious, what
remains is much more glorious. Therefore, since we have such
hope, we use great boldness of speech—unlike Moses, who
put a veil over his face so that the children of Israel could not
look steadily at the end of what was passing away. But their
minds were blinded. For until this day the same veil remains
unlifted in the reading of the Old Testament, because the veil
is taken away in Christ. But even to this day, when Moses is
read, a veil lies on their heart. Nevertheless when one turns
to the Lord, the veil is taken away. Now the Lord is the
Spirit; and where the Spirit of the Lord is, there is liberty.
But we all, with unveiled face, beholding as in a mirror the
glory of the Lord, are being transformed into the same image
from glory to glory, just as by the Spirit of the Lord* (2 Cor.
3:4–18, NKJV).

The good news for us as believers today is that we live under
the New Covenant. We live at the time of the ministry of the spirit
rather than the letter – and that makes the glory fully accessible to us!

We need to invite the Holy Spirit to our meetings in order for us
to enter this place – we have to give Him full access to our hearts.
We can only behold the glory of the Lord through freedom. If we

close the Spirit within the limits of our religiosity, at the same time we close ourselves to commune with God and to know Him in the spiritual realm, which may hinder us from ever tasting the courtyard of heaven.

We can pay a high price for allowing religion to dominate our Christian lives. That is why the next chapter is about religiosity: what is religiosity, how we can fight it and overcome it.

Prayer

(Lyrics: Stacy Swalley)

Just one glimpse of His glory
Just one touch of His hands
And I will never be the same
Cause His spirit keeps flowing through my veins
We sing glory to the Father
Glory to the Son
Holy Spirit fill us up
Till we are one

THINK IT OVER ONE MORE TIME

➢ *What* does the Bible say in 1 Corinthians 2: 9–10? What does it mean for you?

➢ What is the glory of God?

➢ What do you think about your flesh? Is it perfect?

➢ Is it possible to know God at the level of the flesh?

➢ What do you think is the hunger of knowing God? Are you hungry for God? Do you want to be hungry? Why?

➢ *What is the purpose of* the glory of God?

➢ *Do you desire to know* the glory of God? Are you ready for the sacrifice associated with knowing the taste of eternity?

But what do you think? A man had two sons, and he came to the first and said, 'Son, go, work today in my vineyard.' He answered and said, 'I will not,' but afterward he regretted it and went. Then he came to the second and said likewise. And he answered and said, 'I go, sir,' but he did not go. Which of the two did the will of his father?" They said to Him, "The first." Jesus said to them, "Assuredly, I say to you that tax collectors and harlots enter the kingdom of God before you. For John came to you in the way of righteousness, and you did not believe him; but tax collectors and harlots believed him; and when you saw it, you did not afterward relent and believe him. (Matt. 21:28–32, NKJV)

12

THE WALL OF RELIGIOSITY

Religion is the most devastating, paralyzing and limiting
power in the Church today - it is a big wall that cuts us
off from the knowledge of the true God as a Father.

T
he passage quoted on the previous page deals with religiosity
in an amazing way. Perhaps some of us thought the verse in
this line was not in the Scriptures. Perhaps there are those
who doubt whether these words were truly spoken by Jesus. Yes!
Jesus actually said it:

> *Assuredly, I say to you that tax collectors and harlots enter*
> *the kingdom of God before you* (Matt. 21:31, NKJV)

A question arises while reading something like this: Why is that?
Is it possible for such dirty and shameful people to enter the Kingdom
before *me*? Yes, it is possible. That's what Jesus said.

The mystery is that God no longer only expects works in the
New Testament, but He wants our hearts to follow them. The above-
mentioned words are very powerful. In another words Jesus said:
Despite their dirt, imperfection and sin, a true faith was born in their hearts
based on my righteousness, while you still rely on your own righteousness.

Jesus never taught religion or particular rituals - He always pointed to the heart. He said that whatever is on the outside is not as important as the inside.

Humans are prone to evaluate and judge. We think we know when someone is good or bad, deserves God's love or whether we deserve this love ourselves. This looks quite different from the perspective of the Word of God. The heart of man is the place where real love, passion and holiness can be observed. However, only God can see it.

Jesus is our righteousness. He became sin for us so that we can live from His righteousness!

> *For I say to you, that unless your righteousness exceeds the righteousness of the scribes and Pharisees, you will by no means enter the kingdom of heaven* (Matt. 5:20, NKJV)

By this He meant that righteousness is not founded on perfect works but true love that goes beyond outside perfection. On the outside the Pharisees looked impressive. But inside they were filled with death.

Often we confuse two concepts: works for righteousness and works for an award. Good works do not change our righteousness because Jesus Christ is our righteousness. However, they determine what eternity will grant us.

The Father does not look at us other than through the cross of Jesus. If we wanted to show the Lord how righteous we are and for a moment put aside the cross, our holiness would be no more than a dirty rag to God[25]. Thus, the beloved Father sent Jesus to become righteousness for us.

I was raised in a Christian family and attended a conservative church for several years. I heard many sermons on how my life should look like. At my every step they would tell me what I need to do and how should I live my life to please God. A lot was said, in fact, too much.

---

[25]   Isaiah 64

One preacher would say that you should not wear dreadlocks and few weeks later another one would preach that dreadlocks are allowed but ties are not. Eventually, they would change their mind and say you could wear a tie but not dreadlocks. I got a bit lost in all of this.

If we think about what is on the mind of a teenager who is told what he is and isn't allowed to do at every step he takes, we can easily say he wouldn't be thrilled about it. I was sick of it all, not to mention the fact that I got lost in the maze of do's and don'ts.

A few years later, I decided to take things into my own hands and find out what I should really do and how to live a life to please God.

The answer I received completely surprised me. I sensed Holy Spirit words: *I don't demand anything from you.* I was baffled. What do you mean? What about all those rules and forms? What should I choose? What should I do and what shouldn't I do? The answer is eas - *All I want is your heart.*

Yes! That was it. I felt it in a split second. God is not focused on whether or not I wear dreadlocks, walk around during prayer, clap, jump or if I like watching football matches.

My only desire is intimacy with God when He *owns my whole heart.* This is the key to be set free from religion. Nothing and no one is as precious to us as Jesus when we are full of love for the Lord. We can do anything we want, but we are able to give it up at any time because we burn with love for the Lord.

At one of the youth conferences I once heard the following sentence: "The less you sin, the closer you are to Jesus and the more you sin, the farther away you are from Jesus." In reality it does not always work that way. I may not sin; yet live in death, numbness and indifference. But on the other hand, the opposite is always true: "the closer I am to Jesus, the less I sin. The farther away I am from Jesus, the more I sin."

Today, we need to talk more about Jesus, His incredible beauty, His wondrous intimacy and His touch to transform lives rather than hear how little we read the Bible and how sorely little we actually pray. Anyone who rarely reads the Bible knows it very well. But when they hear the story of Jesus and how exciting a relationship with Him can be, surely they will desire to know Him. They will pray and read the Word more[26].

Moralism is not the best way to motivate me. Pointing out the mistakes I have made and telling me how unworthy I am does not bring me closer to Jesus, nor does it reveal even the slightest revelation about His wonderful Person to me.

As it was said earlier, it is not sanctification that guarantees us an encounter with God. It is rather an encounter with God that guarantees knowledge of sanctity and a desire to live a holy life[27].

My pastor used to often repeat the words of St. Augustine: *Love God and do whatever you please.* Yes! This is what Jesus desires for all of us. God does not care about us obeying all the church's rules, observing all the dos and don'ts or becoming an example and displaying excellence in every aspect of life. Jesus has already fulfilled the law – after all, we live in the New Covenant. God mostly cares about love – an attitude which says: *I am wretched, miserable, poor, blind, and naked; I desire Your gold refined in the fire; I want to be hot for You because I do not know You the way I could*[28].

This is the model of New Testament religion. The Holy Spirit wants us to focus on Him, and everything else will be a natural consequence of living in His closeness. It is not possible to truly love and at the same time act against this love. Failure to understand these words is a misunderstanding of the power of love.

Perfectionism is not a biblical model of the Christian life. The Lord does not require us to be perfect in every moment. The Bible says, "become complete"[29]. God does not force us to bear a yoke that cannot be carried. His yoke is easy, light and pleasant!

The Father understands our imperfections. Everyone at times

---

[26] Of course, we must speak about these things, but they can't be the central point of our preaching. The center point is Jesus.

[27] Although, it does not mean we should not take care about our character, purity and morality.

[28] Rev. 3:17, author's paraphrasing.

[29] 2 Cor. 13:11 (NKJV)

makes a mistake or falls. Our Daddy knows this and that is why He primarily looks at what are we going to do with our imperfections rather than whether or not will we have them.

It is as if an earthly father would condemn and beat his son for every little mistake, even a mistake that happened accidently, which the son is not even aware of: spilled cocoa, a shirt buttoned the wrong way or complaining during a meal. We are the children of God and we learn as much as any child. We do not become perfect instantly and we will never be.

Just as we are born in flesh we are also born in the spirit. We are children in the flesh just as we are children in the spirit. You can't require from a child or an infant what you would require from an adult.

Moreover, every one of us considers different things to be *honorable* and *dishonorable*[30]. It all depends on the sensitivity of the human conscience. A canon of dishonorable things that is equal for everyone cannot be established because everyone considers different things to be dishonorable.

The formation of such frameworks is a manifestation of the destructive power of religion. Calling something a sin when it isn't constitutes the worst form of religion and leads to a religious life rather than a life based on relationship. Such life is devoid of any expectations of something more from God. The fulfillment of law becomes the most important, rather than cherishing and developing a relationship with God.

When Jesus spoke of perfection, He did not mean a life free from the imperfections of the flesh but spoke of perfection in love.

> *You have heard that it was said, 'An eye for an eye and a tooth for a tooth.' But I tell you not to resist an evil person. But whoever slaps you on your right cheek, turn the other to him also. If anyone wants to sue you and take away your tunic, let him have your cloak also. And whoever compels*

---

[30]   2 Tim. 2:20 (NKJV)

you to go one mile, go with him two. Give to him who asks you, and from him who wants to borrow from you do not turn away. "You have heard that it was said, 'You shall love your neighbor and hate your enemy.' But I say to you, love your enemies, bless those who curse you, do good to those who hate you, and pray for those who spitefully use you and persecute you, that you may be sons of your Father in heaven; for He makes His sun rise on the evil and on the good, and sends rain on the just and on the unjust. For if you love those who love you, what reward have you? Do not even the tax collectors do the same? And if you greet your brethren only, what do you do more than others? Do not even the tax collectors do so? Therefore you shall be perfect, just as your Father in heaven is perfect. (Matt. 5:38-48, NKJV)

Here, the most important word is "love". Righteousness was most important in the Old Covenant but it is no longer enough in the New Covenant. We need love: *Your perfectness should be based not only on righteousness but on love.* Works that result from righteousness rather than love are not perfection.

Jesus said: *be perfect, just as your Father is perfect. The Puritans usually claim that this passage speaks of perfection in terms of perfect works but Jesus has something different in mind here: He does not want righteousness only - He wants love. Therefore, true biblical perfection lies in love. Sometimes, it is better to express love instead of righteousness to people. We must lose something in order to gain something bigger and more valuable. Religion does not recognize a loss because loss always touches the heart.*

This model of Christianity is not a simpler Christianity but one that is more profound and true. Religion requires superficiality but the Lord looks for the whole heart. Which is easier: performing good works or performing good works *out of love*?

Only the Father knows the true motivation of our hearts because He looks at the heart. However, religion sees superficiality and calls it righteousness. It is so precious to be so close to God, and to be able to see the intentions and motives of your own actions.

Superficiality is one of the main traits of religion. There is a chapter in the Gospel of Matthew that speaks mainly about superficiality.

"Woe to you, scribes and Pharisees, hypocrites! For you pay tithe of mint and anise and cummin, and have neglected the weightier matters of the law: justice and mercy and faith. These you ought to have done, without leaving the others undone. Blind guides, who strain out a gnat and swallow a camel! "Woe to you, scribes and Pharisees, hypocrites! For you cleanse the outside of the cup and dish, but inside they are full of extortion and self-indulgence. Blind Pharisee, first cleanse the inside of the cup and dish, that the outside of them may be clean also. "Woe to you, scribes and Pharisees, hypocrites! For you are like whitewashed tombs which indeed appear beautiful outwardly, but inside are full of dead men's bones and all uncleanness. Even so you also outwardly appear righteous to men, but inside you are full of hypocrisy and lawlessness. (Matt. 23:15-28, NKJV)

It is interesting how often superficiality is identified with the Pharisees. It seems like they are the personification of all religion. But this is not true. There are a number of Pharisees in the Bible who disagreed with religiosity. They knew Jesus, sought the truth and knew that there was something more than just righteousness based on works. They disagreed with a superficial life. Jesus said to one of them, *you are not far from the kingdom of God.* Elsewhere we read about Jesus' conversation with Nicodemus who sought the truth. There were Pharisees who sought and wanted something more.

In the above-mentioned passage of the Bible, Jesus is not speaking to the Pharisees and scribes as those from whom all evil comes, but He spoke to those who were *hypocrites.* In the New Covenant God does not expect only what is outward, but He wants the outward to come out of a heart burning of love.

How is this enforced? There is only one way. We must honestly ask the Holy Spirit to show and reveal to us the true motives of the heart[31]. We do good things very often but we are led by the wrong motives. Our desires are characterized by self-centeredness and thoughts about our own benefits – they do not come from love. We do good things but we think of fame, financial benefits or we long for applause.

Christian hypocrisy is leading a double life – one is for God and the other for men. Hypocrisy is a lifestyle in which living for God is separated from living for men. It is a different standard for life in the Church and life in the world. In a word, it is a requirement of holiness and disregard of love.

1 Corinthians chapter 13 is one of the most recognizable passages in the Bible. It is known not only by Christians but also referred to in literature classes or used in poetry. It also serves as an ornament of wedding celebrations. It is known as the Bible's "love chapter".

This wonderful passage of Scripture points to the most important aspect of a Christian life. Love should be the foundation and pillar of all our plans and activities. Therefore, love is the reason why we need to ponder our own motivations. Is love always the motive for what I do? Does whatever I intend to do come from love? Do I attend church due to love? Do I pray to Jesus with love? Does my fasting come from love for Jesus? Do I sing out of love for Him?

Jesus says, you *strain out a gnat and swallow a camel*. In other words, you talk about excellent deeds and forget about love. That is religion.

Tax collectors and prostitutes knew they lived wrongly. Their awareness of sinfulness made them free from religion. This shows us that despite our spiritual portfolio and merits, we still must be aware of our own weaknesses. This is a wall religion cannot pass.

There is another thing religion is associated with: it humiliates others and exalts itself. I can be sure that I am far from religion if the purpose of my life is to humble myself in people's eyes and exalt my brethren. I have a problem if it is the other way around.

The teachings of Jesus addressed to the Pharisees was concluded

---

[31] Fasting is best tool that makes the flesh weak and causes us to be more sensitive to see real motivations of works, plans and dreams.

by Him in a simple sentence: *I desire mercy, and not sacrifice, these you ought to have done, without leaving the others undone.* We often try to recall the Old Testament time of offering sacrifices and say that cursed is anyone who offers imperfect sacrifices. However, in the New Covenant God does not care for offering sacrifices but *love offerings.* Whatever comes from love destroys all religion. Love is the greatest enemy of religion.

As I talk to people sometimes, I ask them what impresses them the most about Jesus. One person would say what Jesus did for him, how big the sacrifice was and how much He suffered. Then he would start to talk about the things Jesus did in his life. A second person would confess: "What impresses me with Jesus?! The fact that His love is so big! It is His infinite love that led Him to the cross! He loves me so much!" The tears begin to run down his cheeks. And then he would start to say about how wonderful Jesus is. How wonderful His voice is. How much His love is different from the love offered by people.

There is one conclusion. You cannot love and live in a religious world. When someone's life is touched by the love of God, it will be changed forever. This person will always talk about this love and he will live it. His gratitude will reflect the fullness of requited love.

During one of his seminars for married couples, Mark Gungor[32] talked about a frustrated man who was already exhausted by his fruitless, several-years-old relationship and complained that his wife does not understand his needs at all. Mark asked the question: "When was the last time you took her to the theater?" and the man replied: "I do not remember. It was a long time ago." Mark suggested he would do something that would surprise his wife with a vastness of love and creativity - something that will make her love him back.

Given the fact that the man loved his wife, he took the pastor's advice to heart and decided to give it a try. He took his wife to the theater and then he invited her to a nice restaurant for dinner by

---

[32] "Laugh your way to a better marriage".

candlelight. Imagine his surprise when his wife threw herself at him and began to kiss him passionately before they reached home …

We cannot remain indifferent when we learn about the love of God and know what led Jesus to the cross!

Don't forget! Religion is the most devastating power in the Church. It is a huge wall blocking the knowledge of the true God and it limits our Christian life to just a relationship based on a *distance to God* who requires outward perfection. Religion does not know God as Father who really wants our presence and loves us in spite of our imperfections.

Now, let's think about freedom for a moment. Are we called to freedom? The Word of God says so. Lack of freedom is one of the main characteristics of religion. Jesus doesn't free a person *to* sin but sets him free *from* sin.

However, He has something more for us – He wants to release within us an anointing to live *for* Him. We accept freedom *from* sin very often but we are not released to life *for* Jesus.

The idea of freedom was to release man from the bondage of sin so that he would be free to serve God.

Jesus should be in the center of the Christian life, not us. When quality of life rather than Jesus is in the center of our lives it is easy to begin to see God as the One who hates weakness. There is a very fine line between religion and love. The quality of life will always reflect submission to Him when the Person of Jesus is in the center. Consider the following two passages from the Word:

> Oh, taste and see that the Lord is good; (Ps. 34:8, NKJV)
> For I know the thoughts that I think toward you, says the Lord, thoughts of peace and not of evil, to give you a future and a hope. Then you will call upon Me and go and pray to Me, and I will listen to you. And you will seek Me and find Me, when you search for Me with all your heart. I will be found by you, says the Lord, (Jer. 29:11–14a, NKJV)

These verses are the best test for religiosity. We can proclaim Jesus in His beauty, wonder and love or we can preach religion. There is nothing more than this alternative.

I smell religion when I walk into a church and do not hear preaching about the living, real, intimate and loving Jesus. Therefore, placing Jesus rather than me in the center will always be my goal. We should be focused *on Him rather than ourselves*. When we talk about Jesus, people come to Jesus. When we talk about us, people come to us and not Him. Today, we are lacking in preaching about the Person of Christ and not religion.

Motivations associated with the new birth and being the canvas for hours of storytelling is another equally serious issue regarding religion. I had the opportunity to listen to the testimony of a woman quite recently. She confessed her true motivation. She said she grew up in a family where booze parties, one-night stands, profanity, violence and arrogance were part of everyday life. She was raised in an atmosphere of pathology and decadence. One question arose in her heart at a certain point: "Are there still people in this world who have nothing to do with this, who do not drink alcohol, do not smoke and do not curse?" Soon after, she met exactly such people. She accompanied them to the Christian camp and gave her heart to Jesus.

This story would not be a surprise if it were not for the motivation. There are different reasons for people to seek Jesus. Some have had enough of their current life full of pathology and corruption, while others are divorced and look for love. Still others do not find fulfillment in their lives even though they have almost anything.

Whatever lies at the bottom of our hearts will have the greatest impact on what we will receive in life with God. We won't receive anything more if we feel fulfilled. We will never stop crying out that we want to know the Lord better if there is a constant desire for something more at the bottom of our hearts. *Constant lack of satisfaction* is the best motivation for Christians. The greatest cry is: "I want to be even closer to You, my Daddy! Much closer!"

I heard a sermon on the standard of the Christian life when I was in college. I did not have too many A's in school, therefore I was greatly worried. I believed that I was imperfect and that God was not pleased with me. I felt unworthy.

Today, I see it differently. When I think about it: the times of the Old Covenant are long gone and we do not rely solely on perfection, but on love. You can be perfect and still live without love.

Not everyone has the same intellectual potential. We cannot tell somebody: you must be a role model at school because you are a Christian! Jesus does not give us yokes that are too hard to bear. If it were so, the less gifted children, or those from less affluent families would be doomed by definition to God's disapproval. This is simple religious absurdity.

I would have completely missed my calling if I had focused on studying rather than what my heart was telling me. Sometimes perfection is the greatest enemy of fulfilling the calling of God. We have to be vigilant and defend our freedom like lions. We will have to give up perfection for something higher and greater quite often – the response to the Word which the Lord puts on our hearts.

We tread on unstable ground when our motivation is to be perfect in the eyes of men. Today, our wonderful Lord is waiting for those who will consider love for Him to be the highest value and most precious jewel. He is looking for those who will carry a burning desire to know Him even closer and better.

Sometimes it seems to us that we can create love out of good works. But it does not work that way. It is burning love that produces good works. For some, love is devalued and insignificant. This is due to inappropriate role models. Jesus is the highest and most perfect role model of love!

Often, religion makes us do something just because people require this of us. It amazes me how often the fear of accusation and the suspicion of imperfection bring up a sense of duty within us. The Lord wants us to be free from it. He is not a God of fear, but of love and power!

The liberating truth is that no one sees the world pure and clear. Each of us is different and perceives reality in a different way. No one has a perfect and flawless approach. Nobody has a monopoly on doctrine!

The Biblical story of two brothers and their father reveals a very interesting religious attitude. The second part of the parable reads as follows:

> "*But when he was still a great way off, his father saw him and had compassion, and ran and fell on his neck and kissed him. And the son said to him, 'Father, I have sinned against heaven and in your sight, and am no longer worthy to be called your son.'* "*But the father said to his servants, 'Bring out the best robe and put it on him, and put a ring on his hand and sandals on his feet. And bring the fatted calf here and kill it, and let us eat and be merry; for this my son was dead and is alive again; he was lost and is found.' And they began to be merry.* "*Now his older son was in the field. And as he came and drew near to the house, he heard music and dancing. So he called one of the servants and asked what these things meant. And he said to him, 'Your brother has come, and because he has received him safe and sound, your father has killed the fatted calf.'* "*But he was angry and would not go in. Therefore his father came out and pleaded with him. So he answered and said to his father, 'Lo, these many years I have been serving you; I never transgressed your commandment at any time; and yet you never gave me a young goat, that I might make merry with my friends. But as soon as this son of yours came, who has devoured your livelihood with harlots, you killed the fatted calf for him.'* "*And he said to him, 'Son, you are always with me, and all that I have is yours. It was right that we should make merry and be glad, for your brother was dead and is alive again, and was lost and is found.'*" (Luke 15:20-32, NKJV)

How often it appalls us seeing *younger* brothers receiving things from God that we have never received? How often do we judge the lives of others calling them unworthy? How often do we blame God for not granting us the same things that the *younger* ones received despite their bad and immature life? And finally, how often do we fail to use the things available from the Father that are at our fingertips? This is full-scale religion.

We have a loving Father who is full of love! He gives good gifts to *those who ask for them*. The younger son asked and received gifts though he was less worthy – he got them through love and grace.

No person coming to the Lord will be rejected! This is a beautiful truth about our Father. The desiring and asking is more important to your Father than your dignity! Now, say it out loud!

Sometimes I wonder which son was more prodigal: the one who lost his fortune or the one who wasted many years of intimacy with God. Religion is also about wasting what is available for each of us today!

Also, religiosity makes us do something just to receive a reward or avoid punishment. The true and *divine kind of religion* is embedded on the basis of love. Just as there is morality in the natural world, there is also love in the spiritual dimension. This love is the basis for a life with God. In real life we happen to do something out of fear of punishment or hope of reward. But in life with God the order of things is different because morality is not the purpose of the New Covenant. Morality is the fruit of love; however, love is the highest goal[33].

From behind the pulpit I can say: "Brothers and sisters, let us return to morality. Do not lose what should distinguish Christians". Also, I can preach: "Let's fall in love with Jesus! Let's know His heart

---

[33] Of course, I'm not talking about the lack of morality. This would be absurd. Here it talks about morality resulting from love. There is a nominal and literal morality. But there is also a morality resulting from love.

and desire true holiness"[34]! The perfect example here is a spouse who doesn't cheat on his wife just because he is afraid of the consequences, rather than due to his sincere love for her.

True morality only arises in place of the purest love. Thus, we need to fall in love with Jesus so much, so honestly and truly so that literally everything else would lose its value as compared to His love. That is when we can talk about "true morality".

If there is anything we can take from this world, it is love. And if there is anything we can give to the world, it is also love. Therefore, the goal is love, not morality.

The wall of religion arises where there is more of us and less of *God's Word*. We raise another brick to the great wall of religion each time we add to *life* anything that does not flow from the Word of God - we build a bigger obstacle on the way to knowing the true Lord.

The Word is not the letter. The Word is the revelation of the Person of God[35] in His fullness. To love the Word means to first love the One who speaks it to us. We will always be eagerly waiting for His Word when we love Him.

Love for the Word is based on the knowledge of the Shepherd's voice and waiting for His voice and responding to it. A Christian who does not know the voice of God is like a ship without a rudder; abandoned at sea in the midst of the largest storm.

The voice of the Holy Spirit is the carrier of divine life. This voice gives life to what is dead and brings to life whatever does not exist. Without the voice of God, we'll live in a world of religion, following the voice of our own wisdom and routine like blind sheep.

---

[34] I am not in favor of rejecting reproof, chastisement or to teaching proper and good practices, whatsoever. However, I believe that the level of culture and cultivation of good values results from a sincere love that is full of fire for God. I believe that love will never emerge from rules but rules will result and bear the fruit of love.

[35] The Word revealed by the Holy Spirit is always a full manifestation of God. The Word without the revelation of the Holy Spirit is merely the letter of the law and the Bible becomes an ordinary book. John 1:1-3.

The devastating power of religion calls the word something that is just the letter. Religion will always call the Word the letter of the law, while the Word, which is the Lord, will always give life to the letter. That is the difference between religion and relationship. You cannot see the Word while only looking at the letter of the law. It is impossible! There is always life and power in the Word.

Religion imposes burdens hard to bear, sows accusation, brings confusion and extends our distance from God. It causes us to run *from* God rather than *towards* God in a moment of weakness, failure or sin. It kills life and trust, and causes us to miss the things we desire from God in spite of crying out for them.

Limiting the Holy Spirit, taking His liberty away and dictating what He can or cannot do is the worst and the most devastating effect of religiosity.

Religion is the biggest obstacle in the way to the knowledge of heavenly glory. By succumbing to religiosity, we are unable to receive from God anything more than the picture of His image that has been perverted by religion, allows us to have. Thus, it is extremely important to be aware of the big threat that is religiosity.

God wants us to know Him personally. He does not want us to limit ourselves to following His commands; He wants us to be focused on the flow of His life through us. The Lord wants to show us the path of love, intimacy and truly beautiful closeness. This path leads through humility and love by placing the Holy Spirit first. This requires a sensitive heart to what the Word says - a heart that listens to God's Holy Spirit more than to the opinion of man.

Ironically, religion fights against *true holiness* - it makes holiness become a mere fulfillment of rules devoid of a heart full of love.

When we get to know God as our beloved Daddy and Friend, we do not focus on the mistakes that we sometimes make. Getting to know the Lord in His beauty, glory and love is of the greatest importance. Getting to know the Word and not the letter of the law. We move forward regardless of accusations, fears or temporary imperfections. Our heart is burning in love. That is when we know the *courts of heaven* have been opened before us – the place of the mighty glory of God.

As I think about the Church limited and paralyzed with religion, I almost hear the heart of Jesus crying out today for all of us: *Leave religion behind and come to me - come into my marvelous intimacy.* The last chapter will tell us about the courts of heaven – the place where I believe the Lord invites His church today.

Prayer

(Lyrics: *Switchfoot, On Fire*)

They tell you where you need to go;
They tell you when you need to leave;
They tell you what you need to know;
They tell you who you need to be;

But everything inside you knows there's
more than what you've heard;
There's so much more than empty conversations
filled with empty words;
And you're on fire when he's near you;
You're on fire when he speaks;
You're on fire burning out these mysteries;

THINK IT OVER ONE MORE TIME

➤ What is the difference between your righteousness and the righteousness of Jesus?

➤ Has Jesus delivered us *to* sin or *from* sin? What is the difference?

➤ What is Biblical perfection?

➤ What is the difference between the Old and the New Covenant in the perception of good works?

➤ What is the highest standard of morality?

➤ What is the most effective way to fight against religion? What do you think?

How lovely is Your tabernacle,
O Lord of hosts!
My soul longs, yes, even faints
For the courts of the Lord;
My heart and my flesh cry out for the living God.
Even the sparrow has found a home,
And the swallow a nest for herself,
Where she may lay her young—
Even Your altars, O Lord of hosts,
My King and my God.
Blessed are those who dwell in Your house;
They will still be praising You. Selah
Blessed is the man whose strength is in You,
Whose heart is set on pilgrimage.
As they pass through the Valley of Baca,
They make it a spring;
The rain also covers it with pools.
They go from strength to strength;
Each one appears before God in Zion.
O Lord God of hosts, hear my prayer;
Give ear, O God of Jacob! Selah
O God, behold our shield,
And look upon the face of Your anointed.
For a day in Your courts is better than a thousand.
I would rather be a doorkeeper in the house of my God
Than dwell in the tents of wickedness.
For the Lord God is a sun and shield;
The Lord will give grace and glory;
No good thing will He withhold
From those who walk uprightly.
O Lord of hosts,
Blessed is the man who trusts in You!

(Ps. 84:1-12, NKJV)

13

YOUR COURT OF HEAVEN

*One of the greatest desires of the Father for His children
is to reveal to them the courts of heaven – the place where
corruption collides with integrity and temporality with eternity.*

When I think of the words of the Apostle Paul: *For to me, to live is Christ, and to die is gain,* I notice quite an interesting anomaly in myself: I often sigh, longing to be with God already and at the same time I am unsure of what will happen after death. I sing songs that express a longing to be finally found "in this wondrous land where life slowly flows". A place where all problems disappear and tears, pain and suffering are no more. I think of idyll rather than heaven as the presence of Jesus.

Sometimes I think that it is justified but I won't ever agree that my longing for heaven should only be based on a desire to get rid of problems. Such motivation is too simple and universal to be true.

I think that the Father truly wants to offer us a life without problems but this is not the ultimate goal for life in the glory of heaven. The highest motivation for my longing should be living in the full presence of God unlimited by human imperfection. Thus, I will not be focused on problems, but I will mostly think about His glory – the vast, unlimited, wondrous glory of heaven – and this will be my highest motivation.

The most famous Christian prayer includes the following words:

> *Our Father in heaven, Hallowed be Your name. Your kingdom come. Your will be done On earth as it is in heaven. Give us day by day our daily bread.* (Luke 11:2-3, NKJV)

When our Lord passed these words to His disciples, He did not want them to pray, saying: "I don't know what your will *in heaven* is but let it be done *on earth*." Most of all, Jesus wanted the disciples to know about heaven – not just to pray these words only, but in such a way that it would become *their lifestyle*. When we get to know heaven, we are no longer able to pray differently. We cry out to God: *Bring this heaven on earth, O Lord!*

There is only one thing I notice when I think of my youth and the time I was between ten and twenty years old: a huge hunger penetrating my heart. I remember I was desperate and determined. I was ready to do whatever was necessary to encounter the living God. There was a constant cry in my mind: *I want even more of You, Lord! More of You!* Every thought called out: *More of You, more of You!* I repeated it a thousand times and I still repeat it until this day.

When I had a break in my college schedule, I would come to church, fall on the ground and weep in the presence of the Holy Spirit for as long as I could and then quickly return to class. Each moment I had, I used it to spend time with God. At night, after returning from school, I would run to church to cry to God. Sometimes I could not sleep and I prayed until morning. I was desperate to encounter Him and to collide with His glory.

After a few months, a time had come when the power of God would knock me down to the ground within a second, even before I spoke any words of prayer. God literally brought me down and covered me with His glory. I could not stand straight. I completely lost control. The Holy Spirit embraced me entirely, filled my spirit and soul, and poured over my body. I felt I was close to heaven. I was under the impression I was going to die. I felt as though my body would not endure another minute of the enormous heaviness of God's glory.

At that time I was greatly inspired by the story of A. A. Allen, a pastor born in the early twentieth century. The words of his short book became a great encouragement to me as he wrote to constantly seek God and never stop crying out for more. At some point of his life, Allen was so determined to encounter God that he told his wife: *Close the door to the room behind me and do not open it until the Lord comes down to me, there.* It finally happened after a few days – the Lord came and descended upon him in a way he never expected. The pastor described the situation as following:

> *Had my wife opened the door? No, it was still closed! But the light, where was the light coming from? It was then that I began to realize that the light that was filling my prayer closet was God's glory! It wasn't the closet door that had opened, but rather the door of heaven instead! The presence of God was so real and powerful that I felt I would die right there on my knees. It seemed that if God came any closer, I could not stand it!*[36]

That is the glory! This story shows one essential thing: God *always* responds to the hunger of our hearts. The Lord does not give *His glory* away to randomly selected individuals. Neither is He expecting full perfection in the Christian life according to some Puritans' teachings. He wants to see the hunger and burning desire to know Him. He waits for anyone to tell Him, "I will be searching for You until I find You! I will be praying until I know You. I will give up anything to encounter You!"

Since I first encountered God a few years ago, there wasn't a day that I didn't long for that place – there was never a day that I didn't long for the *courts of heaven.*

The sphere of spiritual pleasures arising from the glory supersedes

---

[36] "The Price of God's Miracle Working Power" by A. A. Allen

all the pleasures and sensations of the flesh. We collide with heaven while being in the glory. And the pleasures of the flesh will cease only at the moment of physical death. There is nothing more.

God lets us taste the glory so that we can compare the imperfection of the flesh and the perfection of the spirit. That is the reason why the revelation of the courts of heaven being the place where corruption collides with integrity and eternity collides with temporality is one of the greatest desires of God for His children.

There is a very interesting passage in the Word of God in Psalm 16. David says this:

> *I have set the Lord always before me; Because He is at my right hand I shall not be moved. Therefore my heart is glad, and my glory rejoices; My flesh also will rest in hope. For You will not leave my soul in Sheol, Nor will You allow Your Holy One to see corruption. You will show me the path of life; In Your presence is fullness of joy; At Your right hand are pleasures forevermore.* (Ps 16:8–11, NKJV)

David presents us with a picture of the manifested presence of heaven. For this reason we can understand the effects of the knowledge of the glory of God. First of all, we have unwavering certainty as to our future (shall not be moved), and secondly, we are filled with great joy and peace. This applies to our spirit and soul as well as the flesh. God allows us know the way of life, the fullness of joy and delight which will never cease.

If we compare this picture with many temptations which Christians face, God shows us the difference between the corruptible and uncorrupted or eternal things.

Recently, I heard a story about a believer who fell into alcoholism. Also, I happened to hear about other bondage and addictions of Christians. However, knowing the glory of God we see that whatever the system of the world has to offer is *corrupted*. On the other hand, whatever *uncorrupted* comes only from the presence and glory of God. *Corruption* is always associated with negative consequences for our lives. *Integrity* is joy, peace and pleasure that spreads over our entire being and brings healing changes to whatever needs to be made well.

We read a very similar thing in Psalm 73 written by Asaph.

> *Behold, these are the ungodly, who are always at ease; They increase in riches. Surely I have cleansed my heart in vain, and washed my hands in innocence. For all day long I have been plagued, and chastened every morning. If I had said, "I will speak thus," behold, I would have been untrue to the generation of Your children. When I thought how to understand this, it was too painful for me — until I went into the sanctuary of God; then I understood their end.* Ps 73:12-17, NKJV)

Asaph could not get over the fact that godless people are well, *at ease* and that they *increase in riches*. What we observe here is an incredible fight and struggle in his life. Also, what Asaph also said excites me: *When I thought to know this, it was too painful for me;* (KJV, WEBSTER). When I read this psalm, I see hundreds of thousands of Christians trying to understand why others do better.

The mind is not the best place to obtain the right perspective. There is something much bigger, higher and deeper. A little bit later Asaph says: *until I went into the sanctuary of God,* meaning into the place of the real presence of God. That is when everything has changed. From this moment I no longer needed my mind to understand why the godless are successful. It became simple to me: the greatest wealth lies in the place of intimacy with God.

No treasures of this world or what *only seems to be happiness* are able to match what comes from the place of the real knowledge of the Lord – from the Holy of Holies – the court of heaven.

Man usually sees the concept of pleasure from the perspective of the flesh and considers sexual experiences, stimulants, extreme emotions and adrenaline to give the greatest fulfillment and happiness. But until we know something higher, bigger and stronger (the spiritual realm), our image of pleasure will be very limited.

There is a completely different perspective of pleasure in the *spirit, soul and flesh*, when compared to flesh only. Whenever God comes to us, He touches the entire being. He starts with the spirit, pours Himself on the soul, and saturates all of our thoughts, desires and feelings to finally touch our flesh.

That is the reason for the problems of numerous individuals who have encountered God in a single born-again experience. They recognize the flesh as the only source of pleasure since they do not know the glory of God. This is due to the fact that they are not aware of the spiritual world – fascinating spiritual things – things of heaven that even the angels desire to look into. However, it does not impress those who know God's glory because when we encounter heaven, we become aware of the inferiority of what we experience in the flesh in comparison to the delight of heaven.

Our beloved Father does not want us to wait for death to experience heaven. The Lord wants to lead us into His courts today. He doesn't want us to long for the visible but the invisible for the rest of our life. And this is the heavenly perspective through which we are to see the world around us.

I cried to God for hours, often without sleeping, in fasting and memorizing the Word of God before He let me know the glory in a tangible way and let me into the court of heaven. I did everything I possibly could. I was desperate to know the real Person. I said, "God, come down here and let me know You right now, if You really exist!"

Religion was not attractive to me at the time. I might as well have become a Gnostic or a Jehovah's Witness striving to know God according to a human interpretation arbitrarily imposed, or even thru science. But I wanted to know the *Person*. David says in Psalm 63:

> *O God, You are my God; Early will I seek You; My soul thirsts for You; My flesh longs for You. In a dry and thirsty land where there is no water. So I have looked for You in the sanctuary to see Your power and Your glory.*
> (Ps 63: 1-2, NKJV)

The desire of the heart of David was so great that his body became like a dry and thirsty land where there is no water. And so the matter is very simple here: we must look for the Lord if we want to find Him. If we want to know Him, we must seek Him with all our hearts and confess the words found in the Letter to the Hebrews that says, *the Lord rewards those who seek Him* (Hbr 11:6, ESV).

When Jesus becomes our best friend we will never be able to forget the time when the friendship started. The same is with a human friendship. Someone becomes our best friend when we get to know each other, by shaping a mutual bond and trust. As a result, even after years of separation we still know who and what our friend is like – we know him! We can talk to him about anything, anytime. We know he will always find time for us. That is why it is so precious.

Your court of heaven is not only the place where all the worries of the world die. Your perspective on the perception of your every single problem changes in a moment as you enter that place. You start to look at everything through the eyes of eternity.

It is remarkable that we do not have to worry about how to get there anymore. God offered us his Son whose blood provided us with free and *full* access to the Holy of Holies – heaven. There is no other way in but through His blood.

It is impossible to overestimate the sacrifice of Jesus. Thus, God does not want us to consider heaven as an unfulfilled dream or as something that will happen someday. *Today*, the Lord invites each of us into heaven and to the place where there is absolutely nothing but His presence, glory and power.

I remember one service when a man began to pray very loudly in a foreign language. Later the man said he felt the urgency of the Holy Spirit to do so. An hour later, when the service was over, somebody approached the pastor and said he was very touched by what had happened. He said he is native American Indian and it is impossible for anyone to speak his language here especially since there are only a few dozen of people who use it around the world. The words prayed out loud by the brother were: *Come in, come to my paradise! Come in, come to my paradise!*

Amazing, is not it! The Lord has a place already prepared for each of us in paradise where there is nothing but His manifested presence and glory. God invites you there today. The Lord invites you to know Him in a literal, tangible and intimate way. The road that will take you there goes only through determination and a hunger of the heart.

The wonderful thing about living with God is that He is both great and almighty God and yet loving Father who is very intimate with us. And the fact that He speaks and touches every one of us in a way easy to accept and understand is even more beautiful in our relationship with the Father.

Recently, I visited several different churches. One thing shocked me while visiting them. I realized that today's Christianity, if only based on a dry interpretation of the Word of God imposed by preachers, does not differ from other religions that much. I am no different than the representatives of other religions if I limit myself to listen about God from other people regardless of who they are. I am no different than Mormons, Jesuits or Jehovah's Witnesses if there is no relationship with the *Person of the Holy Spirit* in my life.

The power of the relationship with the Holy Spirit in my life is overwhelming! There are great transformations in my heart as a result of encounters with Him! The power of His words in me is great and powerful!

Also, I have heard stories of people who feel deceived by pastors, leaders, mentors and even prophets as they uttered words that changed the direction of their lives. People made decisions following a *man*. Only after several years they came to the frightening conclusion that they were being lied to! They felt deceived! They became convinced that they have wasted their lives and decided not to have anything to do with the Church!

Many of us can identify with such statements. This situation does not result from the mistakes of pastors, leader or prophets only. The main reason is rather a lack of *personal relationship with the Holy Spirit*. It is sad but very true.

The vast majority of wounds and conflicts in the Church results from the lack of relationship with the *Person of the Holy Spirit*. There is a lack of openness and sensitivity to His voice as well.

Only God may direct my life and man is only a tool that can be used by God to confirm the direction. Only a *relationship with the Spirit* gives me confidence regarding my future.

Recently, a man spoke to me some very unpleasant words. I was greatly grieved and so I quickly confessed everything to the Lord: "Jesus, how can he talk like that – it hurts me, I feel wounded". An then, I sensed very penetrating feeling, it seemed like Holy Spirit was speaking to me: "To be wounded, you have to allow being hurt". [37]

Immediately, I realized that people can hurt us but our reaction to the wounds inflicted will be completely different when we allow God's love to fill us up. There won't be any bit of accusation or bitterness in us. Love and forgiveness will fill us up because the love of God covers all pain and heals all wounds – it is a kind of bandage and *aloe vera* for us.

Therefore, *living in relationship* with the Lord is the essence and foundation of the Christian faith. We will never experience happiness, fulfillment, peace and joy without relationship with the *Person* – we will never know the taste and pleasure of heaven.

The Lord invites each one of us today to start running toward this place and to become like Jacob who wrestled with God. He is waiting for a mighty army of people who will not let go until we are blessed by Him. That is when God will reveal the place of His glory to anyone who will lay hold of Him. He will let us know Him as a beloved Father and as our closest friend; He will lead us into His courts and reveal *heaven* to us.

---

[37] In other words, "It is impossible for the inflicted wounds to have a negative impact on your life when you allow the Holy Spirit to cover you with His love".

Prayer

(Lyrics: *Planetshakers, In the Secret Place*)

In the secret place I find You.
In Your sweet embrace, in the stillness, Lord,
I'm waiting here to hear Your voice calling me
You're drawing me

TAKE ME TO THE SECRET PLACE LORD
YOU'RE ALL I NEED
INTO THE SECRET PLACE LORD

Just one moment here with You means more than anything to me

THINK IT OVER ONE MORE TIME

➤ *Would you* like to be in heaven already? What motivates you?

➤ What do the words of the prayer that Jesus taught his disciples mean: "Your will be done on earth as it is in heaven"?

➤ Do you remember the story of Brother A. A. Allen? Do you also have the same hunger in your heart?

➤ Do you believe you can taste heaven today?

➤ Have you decided to seek your own court of heaven yet?

Epilogue

In the mid-twentieth century Jim Elliot said one of the most moving words for the Christian world: "He is no fool who gives what he cannot keep to gain that which he cannot lose." His words were an expression of the wonderful understanding of eternity, for nothing that comes from this world can be more valuable than what is gained for eternity.

Jim knew he could not take anything from this world with him to heaven. He was totally free from material things, fame and power. He knew that he could not keep or take with him to heaven whatever he could lose on the earth. However, by giving up earthly things he could gain heavenly things – something that he could never lose.

Eternity awaits each of us. It is up to us, meaning our decisions, our hunger and our thirst if our life on earth will become a beautiful prelude to the way of knowing the Lord.

We have a completely different approach to temporality when the image of eternity becomes mature in our heart. That is when we desire to do something with our lives that will pass through the gates of heaven with us. There is no better or higher motivation of the heart than being led by love toward the everlasting presence of God. That is the reason why the Lord is willing to reveal heaven to us.

Jesus does not want us to wait on Him unaware. The Holy Spirit has a life full of personal miracles for each of us – small and insignificant miracles but also unspeakable and great ones. The Lord reveals to us by His Spirit all that He has prepared for us – what eye has not seen nor ear has heard, nor have entered into the heart of man. We really do not need to wait for what comes after death. We can have it today! Is it not exciting?

The Lord desires for us to set out on a journey of *knowing* Him, to lay hold of Him as Jacob did and wrestle with Him until we are blessed – until He lets us know who He really is. When God *blessed* Jacob he said, *I have seen God face to face.* This is the exact blessing the Lord wants for us – to meet with Him face to face.

Many of us do not know God in His true glory. This is because we do not allow God to go beyond our idea of who He really is. The Lord calls us to stop it. It is time to say to the Holy Spirit: "I want more! I want something real and true! Lord, go beyond my limits of imagination about You and tear down my image of You, if necessary. I want to know You the way you really are!"

I experienced many moments of despair and helplessness in my life, because life with God is not a fairy tale in which the Father fulfills whatever we desire. God gives us what He knows is good. However, our job is to be patient, to cling tightly to Him and never let go. We will begin to experience the most beautiful moments on this earth if we show faith, courage and determination. We shall see heaven opened and we will taste the glory of God.

We cannot ever afford to build on what we have received in the past. We are to continuously cry for something *new*. We must not think that we have received everything from God and have gotten to know Him as much as we could. This is not possible! There is always *more*. One of the saddest things we can say to Jesus is: "I do not want anything more."

God not only calls us to experience Pentecost, which is to be filled with the Spirit. Jesus has more for us. The Holy Spirit was not sent so that we would limit ourselves to only one encounter with Him. He desires a life filled with glory for us. He wants to reveal the true image of spiritual pleasure to us. He wants to usher us into the place where the revelation of heaven completely overshadows whatever is of this world and we become aware that heaven is our homeland. Only then will we feel like citizens of the Kingdom.

But only Jacobs may receive all that God has for us - those who have decided to challenge God and wrestle Him until He *blesses* them. Jesus is waiting for the violent today, which will take His kingdom by force, desperation and prayer. God is waiting for people hungry for more, desperate for His love, presence and power.

The Apostle Paul said, "Forgetting those things which are behind and reaching forward to those things which are ahead" (Php 3:13, NKJV). He knew that the worst thing he could do was to stop. He knew that if he stopped, he would not receive anything more than what he received in the past. That is why he confessed: "Not that I have already attained but I press toward the goal for the prize of the upward call" (Php 3:14, NKJV). So the best thing we can do in our life with God is to never stop! Always cry for more!

Do not think you have read this book by coincidence. God is still waiting for you! He is the God of endless second chances. It is never too late for Him! His big plans, prophecies, words and dreams for you are still real! You have read this book because the Holy Spirit is calling for your presence today. Whether or not you let Him draw you to Himself depends on you only.

Only God knows what great power lies in your decision. Only He realizes the great power of prayer in a single sentence uttered to Him in sincerity. Only the Lord knows how great the power of crying for more is.

Remember, it does not matter who you are, were, what you did or what you failed in! Satan will always remind you of your unworthiness. However, the truth is in Jesus. He is the way, the truth and the life. You can trust Him! He is always waiting with His open arms ready to receive you, hug you and embrace you with His wonderful love and give you more and more, and more, and more …

So do not delay! Start the pursuit of your own piece of heaven today. Today is the best day to make this decision. Today is the day to deal with religiosity once and for all. Today is the best day to start crying, "Lord, I will not let You go, unless You *bless* me!"

> *How lovely is Your tabernacle, O Lord of hosts! My soul longs, yes, even faints for the courts of the Lord; My heart and my flesh cry out for the living God. For a day in Your courts is better than a thousand. I would rather be a doorkeeper in the house of my God than dwell in the tents of wickedness.* (Ps 84:1-2, 10, NKJV)

About the author

The Courts of Heaven has been first published on the Polish book market.

Martin has been ministering as a pastor and a teacher in a charismatic church in Southern Poland for ten years. His ministry is saturated with love and respect for the Word of God.

He obtained a bachelor degree in Political Science, master degree from Clark University on Professional Communication, he also got a post-graduate degree in Diplomacy, Pedagogy and master degree in Journalism. Currently he also works as a high-school and university teacher. He has a wife, Alina, and three children: Zara, Joel and Melissa. He resides in Lubin, Poland.

Printed in the United States
by Baker & Taylor Publisher Services

.